*For my husband, Jim, and our daughters, Sam and Julie,
with all my love*

And in loving memory of Aaron and Amy

How to Say It®

When You Don't Know What to Say:

The Right Words for Difficult Times

How to Say It®
When You Don't Know What to Say:

The Right Words for Difficult Times

ROBBIE MILLER KAPLAN

PRENTICE HALL PRESS

Published by The Berkley Publishing Group
A member of Penguin Group (USA) Inc.
375 Hudson Street
New York, New York 10014

Copyright © 2004 by Robbie Miller Kaplan
Text design by Tiffany Estreicher
Cover design by Jill Boltin
Cover art by Felix Sockwell

Prentice Hall Press edition: May 2004

ISBN: 0-7352-0375-X

Visit our website at www.penguin.com

This book has been cataloged by the Library of Congress

Printed in the United States of America

10 9 8 7 6 5 4 3 2 1

Acknowledgments

No book is written without assistance. I am deeply grateful to a group of special people who helped me through some daunting experiences, and I owe them a debt of gratitude: my husband, Jim, who loves and supports me every step of the way, and wonderful friends and family members whose support and love helped me heal: my mom, Jean Miller; my sister, Judy Barclay; Dot Dance; Stephanie Eckert; Dr. Helene Gayle; and Rabbi Mindy Portnoy.

To the memory of both my grandmother, Mollie Weil, and my mother, Jean Miller, who passed along a deep commitment to family and the importance of caring and supporting those in need.

Many thanks to my daughters, Sam and Julie, for their contributions.

A special thank you to my agent, Andrea Pedolsky, who always brings out the best in me.

And to my childhood friend, Stephanie Tesone Palmer, whose supportive conversation sparked the idea for this book.

And to my editor, Michelle Howry, for her belief and enthusiasm in this book.

A special thank you to Dr. Alan Dappen, Rabbi Rosalind Gold, and Betsy Giller, for their expertise and review of the manuscript.

And a bouquet of thanks to many friends and contributors whose personal stories and wisdom helped shape this project: Hope Avery, Jill Avery, Stephanie Barclay, Ellen Blalock, Elissa Buie, Sandy Corish, Christina Davis, Lia Denson, Carroll Ellis, Mary Fairchild, Janice Farr, Elyse Fischer, Maureen Gallagher, Heidi Graff, Sara Grasman, Caitlin Hilber, Robin Joseph, Mara Kamen, Margie Kaplan, Joan Lisante, Susan McCullough, Betty McManus, Mark Ouellette, Nicole Ouellette, Kim Palmer, Ritchie Palmer, Stephanie Palmer, Heidi Poza, Judy Reinecke, Beth Remick, Leslie Rose, Brette Sember, Alissa Shubar, Patty Spencer, Katie Sternberg, Nancy Sullivan, Tina Tessina, Angie Walker, Mike Walker, Dianna White, and Jennifer Willoughby.

Table of Contents

PART FOUR
COMMUNICATING IN THE FACE OF CRIME AND VIOLENCE

PART FIVE
COMMUNICATING ABOUT PERSONAL AND FAMILY ISSUES

Introduction

A beautiful baby boy was born to a couple who had been married ten years. Their joy knew no bounds, but the euphoria was short-lived. Just a few hours after birth, the baby developed breathing difficulties and was moved to the neonatal intensive care unit. The doctors were certain something was wrong with his heart but were unable to make a diagnosis.

The next morning the baby was sent by ambulance to Children's Hospital. The dad went along, and in the early afternoon the mom got the horrifying diagnosis; the baby was not going to live. The cardiologist explained he had been born with hypoplastic left heart syndrome, a congenital heart defect for which there was no repair. The baby was expected to live just a few days, and he died when he was seven days old.

The chief cardiologist and the geneticist at the hospital told the grief-stricken couple that the birth defect was not genetic and it was not something they did or could have prevented.

Just eleven weeks later, the couple was both surprised and elated to learn they were expecting another baby. But this second pregnancy held none of the anticipatory joy. This was long before the proliferation of support groups—it was difficult to find families with similar experiences, and their story was a conversation-stopper. They made many people uncomfortable, and worse, there were new and old friends they never heard from again.

In December of that same year, a beautiful baby girl was born. A neonatologist assisted in the delivery room, and she knew immediately that something was wrong. It was quickly decided to send the baby to Children's Hospital. Despite the astronomical odds against it, she was immediately diagnosed with hypoplastic left heart syndrome. They had never known another family to have two children born with this birth defect. The bereaved parents were told that she, too, wouldn't live for more than a few days. But the hospital offered them some hope the next morning. This baby's heart was slightly more developed, and they wanted to try to reconstruct it into a three-chambered heart. They performed her first heart surgery when she was a day old. But after three surgeries, the surgeon told them the baby's heart was too damaged to repair. She died in the operating room at just eleven weeks.

This is a true story, and those babies were my children, Aaron and Amy, and they were both born in 1981. Their deaths were traumatic, but they taught me how important it is to provide support when someone is dealing with loss, no matter what that loss might be. Research tells us that individuals heal and bounce back faster if they can voice their feelings and feel the support of caring souls. Communications need not be elaborate; notes, visits, and phone calls can help someone through a difficult time. An offer of nonjudgmental listening will ease anyone through the healing process.

Like you, I often hear of family members, friends, co-workers, neighbors, and community members who are dealing with difficult and challenging times. I know firsthand how much they need support, but I also find it tough to say and do the right thing. I have written this book for everyone who has been at a loss for words when they need them most. *How to Say It When You Don't Know What to Say* is an outgrowth of my experiences and the experiences of many others who shared their personal stories. I've gathered constructive verbal, non-verbal, and written communication strategies to help you and those in need work through some of life's most daunting experiences. I've spoken to professionals, experts, and individuals who have gone through these losses themselves. From my discussions I have gathered tips and suggestions on what to say and do, how to say it, what not to say and do, how not to say it, and hundreds of resources to learn more about grief, communications, and every type of loss.

I've organized this information into five sections. Because all difficult experiences involve loss and grief, Part One provides an overview of the process of grief and mourning and details how you can help someone who is coping with loss.

Communications are crucial to the healing process, and Part Two details communication strategies you can use to foster healing. And because it is sometimes best to say nothing at all, you will find dozens of listening techniques and suggestions that will help you encourage grievers to articulate their feelings.

Parts Three, Four, and Five provide specific insight into illness, death, suicide, miscarriage, pet loss, mental illness, nonviolent crime, violent crime, sexual assault or rape, domestic violence, natural disasters, terrorism, legal or criminal problems, infertility, adoption, baby or child with special needs, physical disability, separation, divorce, job loss, financial troubles, caregiver responsibilities, and personal disappointment. Each chapter lists emotions and feelings to anticipate so you'll be aware of a range of responses to each loss. The chapters also offer models of appropriate sentences, letters, and e-mails, as well as what *not* to say to the bereaved. The "Special Situations" sections provide productive suggestions on handling specific "real-life" problems you might encounter. You'll find these in all the chapters except Eleven through Eighteen, which involve criminal, legal, and medical issues. Beyond basic support, these experiences require assistance from professionals.

You have the power to make a difference in someone's life. I continually hear personal stories of how one small act of kindness warmed someone's soul. The memory of that kindness acts like a talisman they reach for time and time again during the grieving and healing process.

You can make a difference, and you can start right now.

Postscript

My life had a happy new beginning—my husband and I had the good fortune to adopt a baby girl born in Korea, and she arrived just six months after our daughter Amy's death. She was a vibrantly happy and healthy baby and the tonic we so desperately needed. She continues to bring us sunshine and brighten our lives. Two years later, we adopted another baby girl born in Korea, and finally this precious jewel made our family complete. Our daughters have been the joy of our lives, and despite the terrible pain and loss, it is hard to imagine a day without them.

COPING WITH LOSS

Loss is an inevitable part of living, and at some point in our lives, we all experience loss. Even if we anticipate loss, whether from illness, death, or job termination, it is still shocking and traumatic, releasing powerful emotions and feelings that compromise our coping skills.

And yet we need to cope if we are to heal. That's where loved ones, friends, colleagues, and community play a crucial role. They provide the short-term and long-term support that will initiate healing and help in reestablishing healthy living patterns.

Part One provides general guidelines on grief and the mourning process, emphasizing dozens of strategies you can use to comfort and help the bereaved. More targeted advice on how you can help others cope with specific difficult experiences is offered in Parts Three, Four, and Five.

ONE

What Is Grief?

UNDERSTANDING THE PROCESS OF
MOURNING AND HOW YOU CAN HELP

"O, grief hath changed me since you saw me last,
And careful hours with time's deformed hand
Have written strange defeatures in my face."

—William Shakespeare,
The Comedy of Errors, Act V, Scene I

GRIEF is a normal and healthy response to loss. Individuals experience grief when something is taken away from them such as a physical loss (death of a parent or a chronic illness) or a symbolic or social loss (bankruptcy or employment termination). Mourning is our reaction to grief; it is the painful process we go through to work through our grief and adapt to the loss. We grieve not just for the death of someone we care deeply about, but for any loss we experience, whether it is our health, a marriage, a relationship, financial stability, a job, or a dream. We mourn for what was and what will never be.

Grief is a numbing ordeal; it might seem surreal to those grief-stricken that the sun continues to rise each morning, it sets every night, and the world goes on about its daily business despite their personal upheaval. The world of the griever has changed, and they will need support to find their place in a new world. This is where you can help.

It is helpful to understand how grief can manifest itself and the negative impact it can have on our physical, emotional, spiritual, and social well-being. It is common for grievers to respond:

- **Physically:** Changes and difficulty in sleeping, eating, taking care of one's health, energy, and one's overall well-being.

- **Emotionally:** Feelings of sadness, anger, guilt, anxiety, confusion, and despair.

- **Socially:** Inability or unwillingness to see family, friends, and other acquaintances; go back to work; look for work; or assume responsibilities for the care of others.

- **Spiritually:** Understanding of the world and their place in it, belief in God, religion, and the possibility that prior spiritual beliefs may have lost their meaning.

The Stages of Grief

There has been extensive research on the stages of grief and mourning and the emotional response to loss. We know grief takes over the body, leaving the griever with a host of troublesome feelings that occur in different stages; response and emotions can be so intense that the griever might feel as if they are going crazy.

Emotions tend to cluster in different stages during mourning. The stages are a normal part of grief, but they are not predictable and individuals do not necessarily go through them in order or experience them just once. Individuals can go backward and forward through the different stages; once one emotion is finished, it's not gone for good. It's important to understand the types of emotions and feelings that might occur; if we know it is normal for the griever to feel different emotions, we take the power and fear away from it.

> ᘐ **There is no "right" way to grieve.**

Dr. Elisabeth Kübler-Ross, an expert on grief, conducted extensive research into death and dying. She described five typical stages of grief people go through following the diagnosis of a terminal illness. Her landmark work has been used and adapted to demonstrate the stages of grief people go through following a serious loss.

STEP 1: DENIAL AND ISOLATION

Immediately after a loss, the body becomes numb, as if it just can't fathom or believe that the loss has occurred. A feeling of serenity or a sense of shock, disbelief, denial, and disorientation occur, protecting the body from a huge emotional upheaval while the loss is being processed.

STEP 2: ANGER

Anger over the loss can be uncontrollable and frightening. The anger can be directed anywhere and at anyone as the griever vents the emotion. The bereaved often question "Why me?" or "Why are others allowed to escape this?"

STEP 3: BARGAINING

For certain types of loss, the bereaved tries to bargain, promising to do something in the future to prevent the loss. They might bargain: "If you let my wife live, I promise to go to church every Sunday" or "If you let me conceive, I promise I will never ask for anything else."

STEP 4: DEPRESSION

Once the bereaved accepts that the loss has happened, the acknowledgment of the loss initiates depression. The bereaved relives the experience over and over again, trying to make sense of it and find an answer to the question, "Why?"

> ॐ When individuals are feeling very down, they tend to isolate themselves. If you are out of touch with a loved one who is going through the grieving process, make a point of reaching out to them; they might be unable to reach out to you.

STEP 5: ACCEPTANCE AND HEALING

Acceptance and healing come months or years after the bereaved is no longer haunted by the loss. With time, most bereaved accept the reality of the loss and heal.

Although everyone grieves in their own way and their own time, many find grief to be a frightening and overwhelming process. They might experience feelings of high anxiety, depression, sleeplessness, exhaustion, loss of concentration, and a host of responses. Many report raw emotions that feel toxic and foreign, unlike anything they have felt before. The griever wonders, "Will I ever get over it?" or "Will I ever be normal again?"

> ᧬ We don't ever get over loss; what we do is work through it. We must do our "grief work," and eventually, many grievers accept their loss.

How We Can Help

It is extremely important that we provide emotional support to individuals experiencing loss. They need us not only during the initial period of loss but also over the duration of the grieving process, which can last anywhere from months to years. And yet many individuals reveal that when they need support the most, they often find themselves alone.

The bereaved report that sharing their loss is particularly difficult when some friends, family members, co-workers, and acquaintances withdraw from them. In the case of a death, loved ones and the community rally around the bereaved in the initial days after the loss, but when the bereaved are in the throes of working through their grief in the months afterward, they find themselves without vital support when they need it most. This feels like yet another series of losses.

Sometimes, even caring and well-intentioned individuals shy away from the bereaved because they feel uncomfortable and don't know what to say or do. **The most important thing we can do for someone suffering a loss is to be there for them, just as we will need help someday when we experience loss.**

Why is it so tough to help someone else with loss? It might be that:

- Grievers, those experiencing loss, remind us of life's fragilities.

- We fear that these frightening types of losses could happen to us.

- It can be downright scary to be in the presence of someone grieving who has such powerful emotions.

■ We have unresolved feelings of loss, and experiencing the feelings related to loss with someone else takes us right back to our own personal loss.

It's helpful to understand that different stimuli trigger varied responses in the bereaved. It doesn't really matter what causes the trigger, the bereaved has little control over their response to it. But this in no way implies that the bereaved no longer have responsibility for *any* actions.

> ↵ The bereaved have very basic needs: companionship, a willing listener, and the privacy to say what they feel without fear of judgment or embarrassment.

Reactions to loss are very personal and quite different for each of us. Over the course of our lives, we will each be challenged by different types of losses. It is sometimes hard to comprehend and put into perspective the terrible sadness and loss of someone who has been laid off from a job when you or someone you care about is dealing with the death of a loved one. And yet we can't begin to compare one person's loss to another's—and we shouldn't. Each of us must express our emotions to heal from our losses, and we deserve the respect, understanding, and support to do that.

It is difficult for anyone to understand a specific loss unless you have experienced it yourself. Even if you have experienced the same event, the meaning of it is unique to each one of us. If you have experienced something different, you can't compare or judge others based on your own experience.

We should encourage the bereaved to articulate their feelings; those who repress and keep their feelings and emotions bottled up might prolong and exacerbate their grief. No matter how raw or painful, it is crucial that we encourage the bereaved to fully experience

> ↵ Always remember that each person is unique and will express themselves in their own way and in their own time.

grief and the resulting emotions, mourning fully the loss. It is only through the experience of grief that we can eventually come to accept our loss.

The Anger Backlash

Although anger is a normal response to grief, when someone is grieving, their anger can be misdirected. It is important to understand that if someone directs their anger at you, you are not at fault. Yet it can be hard not to personalize it.

Realize that there is an underlying cause for their anger, and it is not always evident in how it is expressed. Try to encourage someone who is grieving to vent and redirect their anger in safe ways.

- Suggest they scream or yell in a secure environment.

- Recommend they practice sports and physical movement such as aerobic exercise, kickboxing, and martial arts, as these affect mood and help deal with biochemistry gone amuck; but realize that everyone is different and each person needs to find what works best for them.

- Encourage them to explore the arts such as reading poetry and books, playing or listening to music, or writing a journal or other written form of expression.

- Recommend punching a pillow or putting on boxing gloves and punching a bag to let off steam.

- Encourage them to eat well and take care of their physical well-being.

Above all, the bereaved will need to tell their story over and over again. Your gift of patient listening is what they need to facilitate the healing process. In the next chapter, we'll discuss specific words you can say and ways you can communicate that comfort and heal those going through difficult times.

For further information:
Attig, Thomas. *How We Grieve: Relearning the World*. New York, NY: Oxford University Press, 1996.

Canfield, Jack, and Mark Victor Hansen, eds. *Chicken Soup for the Grieving Soul: Stories About Life, Death, and Overcoming the Loss of a Loved One.* Deerfield Beach, FL: Health Communications, Inc., The Life Issues Publisher, 2003.

Cobb, Nancy. *In Lieu of Flowers—A Conversation for the Living.* New York, NY: Pantheon Books, 2000.

Deits, Bob. *Life after Loss: A Personal Guide to Dealing with Death, Divorce, Job Change, and Relocation.* Tucson, AZ: Perseus Publishing, 1999.

Hickman, Martha Whitmore. *Healing After Loss—Daily Meditations for Working Through Grief.* New York, NY: HarperCollins Publishers, 1994.

James, John W., and Russell Friedman. *The Grief Recovery Handbook: The Action Program for Moving Beyond Death, Divorce, and Other Losses.* New York, NY: HarperCollins, 1998.

Kübler-Ross, Elisabeth, and David Kessler. *Life Lessons: Two Experts on Death and Dying Teach Us About the Mysteries of Life and Living.* New York, NY: Touchstone Books, 2002.

Mabey, Juliet, comp. *Words to Comfort, Words to Heal—Poems and Meditations for Those Who Grieve.* Oxford, England: Oneword Publications, 1998.

Moody, Raymond, Jr., M.D., and Dianne Arcangel. *Life After Loss—Conquering Grief and Finding Hope.* New York, NY: HarperCollins Publishers, 2001.

Prend, Ashley Davis, A.C.S.W. *Transcending Loss: Understanding the Lifelong Impact of Grief and How to Make It Meaningful.* New York, NY: The Berkley Publishing Group, 1997.

American Association of Retired Persons (AARP) Grief and Loss, a collection of resources, a community of care
www.aarp.org/griefandloss/

GriefNet.org is an Internet community of persons dealing with grief, death, and major loss with forty-seven e-mail support groups and two websites.
www.GriefNet.org

Especially for children:

Doka, Kenneth J., ed. *Living with Grief—Children, Adolescents, and Loss*. Washington, DC: Hospice Foundation of America, 2000.

Emswiler, Mary Ann, M.A., M.P.S., and James P. Emswiler, M.A., M.ED. *Guiding Your Child Through Grief*. New York, NY: Bantam Books, 2000.

See also: WHAT CAN I SAY? COMMUNICATIONS THAT COMFORT and WHAT CAN I DO? HOW TO LISTEN.

BASIC COMMUNICATIONS

Your instinct might be to avoid someone who is experiencing loss because you fear you'll say the wrong thing. But loss can be very isolating, and if you stay away, you will compound the loss and the pain.

Communications can be the tonic individuals need when experiencing loss, and comforting communications can play a vital role in the healing process.

But words alone won't help those experiencing loss. Their complicated and sometimes contradictory feelings must be articulated if they are to work through their grief. In addition to comforting, you can help in another way, too—by listening.

Part Two gives general guidelines on verbal, written, and nonverbal communications that are sure to comfort. It offers models of what to say as well as what not to say to the bereaved. You'll also learn techniques for listening, which is sometimes the most effective communication of all. More fine-tuned advice is offered in Parts Three, Four, and Five as it relates to specific difficult experiences.

TWO

What Can I Say?

COMMUNICATIONS THAT COMFORT

*"Our words are useless unless they come from
the bottom of the heart."*

—Mother Teresa

WORDS are powerful, and we are often unaware of the consequences our words can have on someone experiencing or suffering a traumatic event. Despite intentions to comfort or console, we might inadvertently say something that truly hurts or angers someone we care about. No matter how well meaning we are, we can easily increase someone's suffering by thoughtless and inappropriate statements and actions. How we communicate with those around us experiencing difficulties or tragedies can positively or negatively impact the individual's recovery as well as make or break the future of our relationship with them.

Individuals experiencing trauma must deal and react to myriad emotions. They are feeling overwhelmed and frightened. It is possible that they themselves don't understand what they are going through. In this state, it is normal to suffer conflicting emotions and easy to feel isolated.

Medical and mental health professionals use timetables to predict healing stages. These might be useful clinical guidelines, but in truth, they are just that—guidelines. We all have our own timetables—life is lived outside a textbook, and stages are not always predictable. It is essential that we not judge others by their ability and timeliness in coping and healing.

The greatest gift you can give someone experiencing a trauma is love and acceptance, no matter what they might be feeling. Everyone responds to traumatic situations differently; whatever they feel or do is the right thing for them.

Despite your best intentions, you might shy away from supporting someone who is dealing with a situation that is beyond anything you have personally experienced. You might be afraid to communicate, fearful that you might hurt rather than help. Don't allow your lack of experience to suppress your good intentions. Just be honest and tell them, "This is a journey I have yet to take or understand. I want to be there for you, and if I say something inappropriate, you can let me know."

Keep in mind that even the simplest words and gestures bring solace. You'll find inspiration in the dozens of potential words and phrases that follow, along with plenty of ideas and specific tips for crafting written, spoken, and electronic communications that are sure to comfort.

WHAT TO SAY AND DO

- *Become a sympathetic ear.* Be willing to listen attentively, without giving advice or opinions.

- *Be a support system.* Let the speaker know that you will be available to support them through this difficult time.

- *Time your communication.* Choose a time to interact that is private.

- *Be specific in asking what you can do and offer to help.* Clearly state what you would like to do to help, such as taking over the carpool for the week or bringing over a dinner on Thursday. Don't wait for them to come to you for help. When you say "Call me if I can do anything," you are transferring the burden to someone who is having difficulty coping. When you offer, you accept the burden, and the recipient will be most grateful.

> ꝏ If you are at a loss for what to do or say, you can simply say "I am so sorry for your loss" or "I am so sorry this has happened."

- *Be persistent, but not annoying, in offering help.* Some folks are so afraid of being a burden or appearing needy that they refuse offers of help even when they need it. Don't worry about rejection, and continue to keep in touch and remain a presence in their life.

- *Listen without judging.* Foster an atmosphere that promotes understanding and open communication.

- *Don't be afraid to touch.* Touch is therapeutic, but before touching, take your cues from the person experiencing the loss. A light touch on the arm or hand can comfort without infringing on the recipient's personal space.

- *Find common ground.* You might have been through something similar that you rarely share that might make the individual feel less isolated and more hopeful of healing. Share your personal journey, but be careful the dialogue doesn't shift the focus to you.

- *Be in attendance—at the hospital, wake, funeral, or at home.* Your physical presence is a comfort and support.

- *Write notes and send cards.* Notes and cards become personal keepsakes, and many recipients reread them when their spirits sag.

- *Bring a meal.* It's okay to bring comfort foods, even if you are told nothing is needed. Bring something that can be placed in the freezer for a future date.

- *Be there and support the person when they need to cry.* Don't be intimidated by tears—they are a healthy response to grief and loss.

- *Allow yourself to cry with the person.* You have feelings, too, and it's okay for you to express them.

- *Keep in touch by phone, mail, and e-mail.* And *stay* in contact—most contact is made at the beginning, but you will be needed for the long term.

- *Remember important dates.* Recipients will be most appreciative if you remember them at significant anniversaries such as the date of birth, death, or surgery, as well as holidays.

- *Listen attentively, even if you have heard a story a dozen times.* Talking is essential to the healing process, and individuals need to share their story again and again. This is one way to try and make sense of what has occurred.

- *Offer to do specific tasks.* Individuals might be so overwhelmed it may be impossible for them to single out specific chores. If you take the initiative it will significantly lighten their burden.

WORDS TO USE

Brave	Heartfelt	Remembrance
Cherish	Heartrending	Respect
Comfort	Heartsick	Saddened
Compassionate	Honor	Share
Condolences	Hurt	Shocked
Console	Inspirational	Sincere
Courage	Keepsake	Solace
Courageous	Lasting	Sorrow
Ease	Legacy	Sorry
Embrace	Loss	Spiritual
Enriched	Memorial	Strength
Eternally	Memories	Sustain
Eternity	Miss	Sympathy
Everlasting	Mourn	Thoughts
Faith	Offer	Touched
Forever	Pain	Tribute
Friendship	Painful	Understanding
Grieve	Peace	Unforgettable
Hardest	Prayers	Uplifting
Heart	Praying	Weather
Heartbroken	Regard	

PHRASES TO USE

Deeply saddened	My heart aches
Ease your pain	Our thoughts are with you
Left their mark	Remembered with love
Made a difference	Sending loving thoughts
May love sustain you	Thinking of you
May you find peace	This difficult time
May you gain strength	This sad time

We share your grief

We share your sadness

We will always remember

We will never forget

With deep sympathy

Words are inadequate

Words cannot express

Words escape me

Your great loss

HOW TO SAY IT

How very sad I was to hear that you are going through such a difficult time.

How very sad we were to hear of your loss.

I am here, and I want to listen.

I am here to listen if you want to talk.

I am sad for you.

I am so sorry you are faced with such sorrow.

I am sorry.

I know how it feels to have no one know how you feel.

I will never forget her.

I would like to bring you lunch; which is better for you, Monday or Tuesday?

I would like to pick you up and take you out to lunch.

Is there something I can read so I can understand what you're facing?

It must be difficult to go through this.

May your fondest memories of her comfort you always.

May your memories be everlasting.

May your memories be sweet and everlasting.

May your memories fill your heart with love and peace.

Memories of our friendship have flooded my thoughts and touched my heart.

My heart aches for you.

My love and prayers are with you.

My sympathy and thoughts are with you.

My thoughts are with you during this difficult time.

My thoughts are with you during your time of sadness.

Our hearts go out to you.

Our thoughts and hearts are with you in your great sorrow.

Our thoughts are with you.

Please accept my sincere condolences.

Please know how much I care.

Please know that our sympathy and thoughts are with you.

Take all the time you need.

There might not be a reason we can understand for everything that happens, but if we look carefully, whatever happens is generally full of meaning.

We hope you will feel some comfort knowing your grief is shared by so many friends.

We share your loss and grief.

We will always remember him with happy memories.

We will keep you in our thoughts and prayers.

Words cannot express how sad I feel for your loss.

You continue to be in my heart and prayers.

Your loss is unimaginable.

WHAT NOT TO SAY AND DO

- Don't force your religious views or opinions about afterlife on the ill or bereaved person.

- Avoid inappropriate statements such as "It's a blessing in disguise."

- Don't give your unsolicited opinion on what they should do, such as "You have no choice but to have the surgery."

- Don't downplay the severity of their illness or their feelings.

- Don't try to change their feelings.

- Don't try to lighten the mood when someone is crying by saying something to initiate some laughter. Although laughter might feel good for the moment, the individual who is crying might think you are uncomfortable with their crying and prefer that they stop.

- Don't think you are commiserating by sharing your own aches and pains.

- Don't compare your pain and experience to the person who is grieving; you can't possibly know what this person is experiencing, and they need your comfort, not a comparison.

- Avoid any statements that minimize the problem such as "You must be relieved it is over."

- Don't use judging statements such as "It's time to be over this."

- Avoid any statement that makes them feel guilty for feeling so bad, such as "Other people have it worse than you."

> ॐ Pay special attention to individuals who are not crying or demonstrating emotion. Just because they are not articulating their grief doesn't mean they are okay. Everyone who experiences loss needs our support, especially those who keep their emotions to themselves and have difficulty vocalizing their feelings.

- If you have listened, said, and done all the comforting things and the person opens up and shares their experience and feelings, don't ignore or avoid them in the weeks ahead. If you do, it will embarrass them and make them feel that they made a mistake by trusting and confiding in you.

HOW NOT TO SAY IT

I really believe things happen for a reason.

If something had to happen, this isn't so bad.

It could have been worse.

It won't happen again.

It's all for the best.

Look on the bright side.

Maybe this is the way it's meant to be.

Perhaps it is better this way.

Put it behind you.

How to Communicate in Writing

It's sometimes hard to speak with family members, friends, neighbors, colleagues, or acquaintances when we learn they are experiencing adversity. It's not that we don't care, but we might be afraid we'll say the wrong thing and hurt, rather than help. Or someone we care about might be too difficult to reach or a phone call might be inappropriate.

If you are uncomfortable or unable to place a call, a personal message in the form of a card, note, or letter is an excellent way for you to communicate and let them know you care. Electronic mail is another option. Although it is less personal than a letter, its rapid delivery and around-the-clock accessibility make it a perfect match for individuals too busy to call or write, users seeking frequent contact, or those who fear phone calls might disturb the recipient. It's particularly appealing for those located out of town, as electronic mail is free to send and an easy way to keep in touch.

Here are some tips and suggestions to help you craft thoughtful electronic and written messages:

- It is best to compose your electronic message and let it sit for a short while to ensure it conveys what you would like to say. It is very tempting to draft your message and press the "send" key, but once it is sent, it is too late to make any changes.

- Personal written messages should include the date, salutation, paragraphs, complimentary close, and your signature.

- Most personal notes are handwritten, but if you are more comfortable writing at your computer or your handwriting is difficult to read, it is also fine to send a typewritten message. Just be sure to sign your name at the end.

> ☞ Sympathy notes are treasured remembrances and are often saved. They become tangible reminders of how others care for us, and they often help us deal with loss.

- If you are writing to a colleague who might not know your home address, include it on the outside of your envelope so they can reach you if they desire.

- It might be helpful to draft your message first, edit and make changes, then write your final note or e-mail.

- You might want to wait a day or more before drafting your message to digest the news and collect your thoughts; it is helpful to have time to process the loss or difficulty and decide what you would like to say.

> ☞ The individual or family will most likely be distracted and taking care of the business at hand. They will not be upset if they don't hear from you immediately. In fact, they might get a lot of mail initially. They'll have more time to read a note from you a few days later, and they might appreciate the distraction.

- If you do choose to write immediately, let your note or message sit overnight and read it again before mailing it to ensure it makes sense and communicates the message you would like to convey.

- Use postcards for quick communications when you just want to keep in touch. They are easy to collect in your daily travels and are a terrific and easy way to reach out to someone whose life has turned upside down. A short note such as "I hope this is a good day for you" or "Thinking of you and sending some sunshine your way" will brighten the recipient's day.

- If your brain goes numb when you attempt to write, purchase thinking of you or sympathy cards; but a card with just your signature is so sterile that you'll add more meaning with a handwritten line or two.

Special Situations

When something bad happens to someone I care about, I say nothing because I am afraid I will say the wrong thing.

If you say nothing, you send a message that you don't care or the experience makes you so uncomfortable you'd rather stay away. It's important to be in touch with people you care about, and it's better to just let them know you care and are thinking about them than to avoid contact.

A friend of mine suffered a terrible loss. I made contact with her initially, but I have not heard from her since and am very afraid that I might have said the wrong thing.

Your friend might be overwhelmed with her grief and unable to respond to you. It is appropriate to follow up either by a note to let her know that she is in your thoughts or with a telephone call. She might respond or not, and either is okay. When you reach out to someone suffering a loss, you are giving them a gift of yourself and you should expect nothing in return. So don't take a lack of response personally; they received your message of your caring and concern, and that was your purpose. If at some point you learn that you said something that hurt her, just move on. Relationships are ongoing, and you get a chance to do it again; just continue to maintain contact, and keep the door open for when she is feeling better.

For further information:

Baugh, L. Sue. *How to Write First-Class Letters.* Lincolnwood, IL: NTC Publishing Group, 1994.

Bridges, John, and Bryan Curtis. *A Gentleman Pens a Note—A Concise and Contemporary Guide to Personal Correspondence.* Nashville, TN: Rutledge Hill Press, 2003.

Kushner, Harold S. *When Bad Things Happen to Good People.* New York, NY: Avon Books, 1997.

Maggio, Rosalie. *How to Say It.* Paramus, NJ: Prentice Hall Press, 2001.

Olen, Dale R., Ph.D. *Communicating—Speaking and Listening to End Misunderstanding and Promote Friendship.* Holmes Beach, FL: Learning Publications, 2002.

Sell, Colleen. *A Cup of Comfort.* Avon, MA: Adams Media Corporation, 2001.

———. *A Cup of Comfort for Inspiration.* Avon, MA: Adams Media Corporation, 2003.

Shepherd, Margaret. *The Art of the Handwritten Note.* New York, NY: Broadway Books, 2002.

Spitzman, Robyn Freedman. *When Words Matter Most.* New York, NY: Crown Publishers, Inc., 1996.

Venolia, Jan. *The Right Word! How to Say What You Really Mean.* Berkeley, CA: Ten Speed Press, 2003.

American Self-Help Group Clearinghouse
www.selfhelpgroups.org
A keyword-searchable database of more than 1,100 national, international, model, and online self-help support groups for addictions, bereavement, health, mental health, disabilities, abuse, parenting, caregiver concerns, and other stressful life situations.

Especially for children:
Coleman, Dr. Paul. *How to Say It to Your Kids.* Paramus, NJ: Prentice Hall Press, 2000.

See also: WHAT IS GRIEF? UNDERSTANDING THE PROCESS OF MOURNING AND HOW YOU CAN HELP and WHAT CAN I DO? HOW TO LISTEN.

THREE

What Can I Do?

How to Listen

*"Wisdom is the reward you get for a lifetime of listening
when you'd have preferred to talk."*

—Doug Larson,
United Press International

Iɴ the last chapter, I discussed some general techniques for talking with some-one who has faced a loss—words you can use, phrases you can express, and thoughts you can communicate to ease their pain. But often, saying absolutely nothing—just being there to listen—is the single most important thing you can do to help.

Most of us yearn to share our feelings and thoughts with someone who will really listen, and yet we are often disappointed. When someone is troubled and experiencing difficult and challenging times, they want someone to understand and appreciate what they are going through. Their needs are really quite simple; they are just looking for comfort.

When we listen, we give the speaker something quite special—a gift of our time and attention. Listening allows the speaker to vent feelings and emotions. By giving a voice to their problems and difficulties, the speaker can sort through issues, challenges, and alternatives, often discovering answers and potential so-lutions by themselves.

Difficult experiences can leave us feeling lonely and isolated. An effective lis-tener can ease someone's suffering and promote healing. The best listeners are empathetic or have prior experience with similar grief. They have the unique ability to put themselves into someone else's shoes and experience so they appear to know how that person truly feels. An empathetic listener is the first aid someone needs while dealing with a difficult and challenging situation.

How Do I Listen?

Listening is neither innate nor automatic. It is both a skill and a discipline, and it must be learned. Like any skill or discipline, it takes practice and self-control to become proficient.

Although listening is the most frequently used form of communication, you won't find it taught like reading, writing, and speaking. Listening is the primary key to effective communications, but you'll need to be self-motivated to develop your own techniques to acquire, practice, and master this skill.

Many people think that "hearing" is the same thing as "listening," but it's not. Hearing is the physical part of listening, when your ears first sense sound waves. After we hear, we interpret what is being said. Next, we evaluate the information, and finally, we react to what has been said. This interaction is essential to listening. Good listeners foster the silence necessary to encourage speech.

It is easy to find talkers—everyone seems to have something to share and wants to be heard. But if we are continually talking, we can't possibly be listening. And when we do take the time to listen, most folks act like it is something for them to do while waiting their turn to speak.

When someone thinks enough of you to share their burden, they are seeking an outlet to articulate their feelings and troubles. This is referred to as cathartic communication. You are being asked to listen and nothing more; no one expects you to have the answers, and no one wants you to judge.

Your job as a listener is quite simple: You are to listen and allow the speaker to feel, whether it is anger, pain, or fear.

> ♾ Listening is not a passive activity; it takes energy, and it is hard work.

It is not your job to teach, to influence, to direct, or to correct; it doesn't matter how you think or feel. What is important is to allow the speaker to vent. Whatever emotions the speaker experiences are normal. Emotional release is a good thing and vitally important in the mourning and healing process.

ॐ **Don't take anything personally. This is not about you but about the person who is hurting.**

There are a number of things you can do to show that you're an active, engaged listener.

WHAT TO SAY AND DO

- Choose a setting that is quiet; one that is comfortable and private is even better.

- Look directly at the speaker.

- Tilt your face toward the speaker.

- Lean toward the speaker.

- Use body language.

- Mirror the body language of the speaker.

- Make eye contact.

- Employ facial expressions.

- Restate words and messages when appropriate.

- Open your posture.

- Be calm.

- Be patient.

- Demonstrate warmth.

- Disregard your own needs, and concentrate on the speaker.

- Allow the speaker to experience their feelings rather than you anticipating or guessing what they are feeling and putting words in their mouth.

- Train your eyes to look for nonverbal signals.

- Send out your own nonverbal signals, such as nodding your head, that indicate you are actively listening.

- Stop talking.

- Avoid interruptions.

- Open your mind to concentrate so you can hear what the speaker is conveying.

- Allow the person to talk as much as they need to, even if they ramble and don't make sense. It is the telling and retelling that will enable them to discover for themselves what is going on in their life and the meaning of those experiences.

- Change the way you are sitting if you feel yourself begin to slip away during the conversation.

- Encourage the person to talk more by asking open-ended questions, one at a time.

- If you are reaching out to them by telephone, make sure you have enough time to listen before placing the call.

> ℅ Ending an emotional conversation can be awkward. Wait until there is a real lull in the conversation and say, "I'm really glad we had this chance to be together. Is it okay if I visit you again soon? (or call you again soon?)"

- Graciously accept their appreciation by telling them it makes you feel good to be able to help in some way.

- If the person cries or has no words, just listen. Assure them that they should take all the time they need before continuing the conversation.

HOW TO SAY IT

I can see that you feel strongly about that.

I can understand how you can see it like that.

I can understand how you might feel that way.

I can't be in your shoes, but I can be by your side and listen.

I can't say I've been there, but I've been in the neighborhood.

I see.

I understand.

If you want to talk, I'm here for you no matter how you need me.

Thank you for trusting me enough to share your feelings.

Would you like to talk about it?

WHAT NOT TO SAY AND DO

- Don't assume that you know what the speaker thinks or feels.

- Don't multitask—save the knitting or mail-sorting for later.

- Don't look away from the speaker.

- Avoid crossing your arms or legs.

- Don't roll your eyes.

- Avoid tapping your fingers, cracking your knuckles, or cleaning your fingernails.

> ॐ **Turn off your cellular phone; a ringing phone will interrupt the speaker's thoughts and might conclude the conversation.**

- Don't interrupt.

- Don't take it personally if anger is expressed.

- Don't abandon someone because they are angry and need to vent their emotions.

- Don't yawn or nod off.

- Don't shake your head.

- Don't rush the speaker.

- Don't get ahead of the speaker and finish their thoughts.

- Don't ask questions about the details; allow them to express and share that information with you if or when they are ready.

- Don't cut them off before they have finished expressing themselves.

- Don't tell your own stories; this is not about you.

- Don't tell stories about people you know or things you have read or heard about; their story is unique and all their own.

- Don't change the subject when the speaker takes a pause.

- Don't judge them for what they have expressed.

- Don't tell them what to think or feel.

- Don't try to solve their problems.

- Don't offer advice.

HOW NOT TO SAY IT

I know just how you feel.

If you think that's bad, wait until you hear . . .

I'm sorry you feel that way.

My sister (mother, father, brother, cousin, neighbor) had the same thing happen.

So what are you going to do about it?

That reminds me of . . .

That's nothing, let me tell you about . . .

You should be happy; things could be a lot worse.

You shouldn't feel like that.

For further information:
Barker, Larry, Ph.D., and Kittie Watson, Ph.D. *Listen Up: How to Improve Relationships, Reduce Stress, and Be More Productive by Using the Power of Listening.* New York, NY: St. Martin's Press, 2000.

Burley-Allen, Madelyn. *Listening: The Forgotten Skill: A Self-Teaching Guide.* New York, NY: John Wiley & Sons, 1995.

Kratz, Dennis M., and Abby Robinson Kratz. *Effective Listening Skills*. New York, NY: McGraw-Hill, 1995.

Nichols, Michael. *The Lost Art of Listening: How Learning to Listen Can Improve Relationships*. New York, NY: The Guilford Press, 1996.

Shafir, Rebecca Z. *The Zen of Listening: Mindful Communication in the Age of Distraction*. Wheaton, IL: Quest Books, 2000.

International Communication Association
1730 Rhode Island Avenue, NW, Suite 300
Washington, DC 20036
(202) 530-9855
www.icahdq.org

International Listening Association
(800) ILA-4505
(715) 425-3377
www.listen.org

See also: WHAT IS GRIEF? UNDERSTANDING THE PROCESS OF MOURNING AND HOW YOU CAN HELP and WHAT CAN I SAY? COMMUNICATIONS THAT COMFORT.

PART THREE

COMMUNICATING IN TIMES OF ILLNESS AND DEATH

Illness and death bring unwanted change—change that shakes an individual's confidence, disturbs their life, interrupts their routines, and leaves them feeling vulnerable. And in this state of confusion and vulnerability, they must make major decisions while taking care of their lives and their households.

You can play a major role in helping your loved one, friend, coworker, or community member cope with illness and death. Your presence and support can guide and lead them through this traumatic period.

Part Three provides specific insight into illness, death of an adult, death of a child, birth of a stillborn or death of a newborn baby, suicide, miscarriage, pet loss, and mental illness, with guidelines on verbal, written, and nonverbal communications you can use to comfort.

FOUR

Illness

"Happiness, grief, gaiety, sadness, are by nature contagious. Bring
your health and your strength to the weak and sickly, and so you will
be of use to them. Give them not your weakness, but your energy, so
you will revive and lift them up. Life alone can rekindle life."

—Henri-Frederic Amiel

AT some time, we all encounter a sick or ailing family member, friend, neighbor, colleague, or acquaintance. When someone we care about is in physical and emotional pain, we suffer along with them. Whether the illness is acute
(short term), chronic, or terminal, it takes a physical and emotional toll. You
can't fix the physical, but your words and nonverbal actions can significantly aid
the emotional recovery and healing process.

Each of us is unique, and we each deal with diagnosis and treatment in our
own way. The person you care about can be experiencing a variety of emotions
at any given time. Diverse stimuli, encounters, and experiences trigger these responses, and during the course of recovery and healing, one can succumb to and
resolve these feelings any number of times.

Your personal experience with illness, hospitalization, or similar situations
will influence your feelings and emotions—and impact your ability to help and
support others in need. If you've had a bad experience and find going to the hospital to visit a friend a hard thing to do, it's okay if you don't go—but plan to
make contact in another way. Use past experience as a guide to extend comfort;
offer what made you feel better or things you wished others had done for you in
a comparable situation.

No matter what you choose to do, keep in mind that different people need different things. Some folks like to be fussed over, and others prefer to be left alone. It will be your job to discover what works for each person.

THINGS TO CONSIDER

- Whether the illness is acute, chronic, or terminal.

- The person's physical condition and ability to communicate.

- Their emotional well-being.

- Their desire to interact.

- Whether they have family or loved ones living with them or nearby.

EMOTIONS AND FEELINGS TO ANTICIPATE

- Anger
- Devastation
- Disorientation
- Fear
- Frustration
- Grief
- Guilt
- Helplessness
- Loss
- Paralysis
- Self-blame
- Self-devaluation
- Self-pity
- Shame

GUIDELINES FOR VISITING SOMEONE WHO IS ILL

- Direct the conversation to focus on the patient; it is not appropriate to discuss your personal or health issues.

- Limit your hospital or home visit to ten to fifteen minutes. Patients might not have the energy for a longer visit in the early stages of illness but might appreciate more of your time as they convalesce. Take your cues from the patient to determine if they are up to a longer visit.

- Don't ask intrusive questions about their prognosis, treatment, or frailties.

- Do ask questions that show interest and leave the door open for the patient to share their health situation with you such as "How are you?" or

"How are you feeling?" If the patient is in the hospital, ask, "What are they telling you about when you'll get to go home?" or "How long will your hospital stay be?"

- Bring something for them that requires little attention, such as a potted plant, flowers in a vase, a cheerful helium balloon, a framed photo, a stuffed animal, a book on tape or CD, or a book to read. Only bring a spiritual item if you know this would be appropriate.

- Don't bring cut flowers that need to be arranged or a fussy plant that requires special attention.

- Do take your cues from the patient in conversing.

- You can ask "Is there someone you would like to see?" and you can make the contact.

WHAT TO SAY AND DO

- Ask if you can set up a phone tree to update family and friends so they won't barrage the household with extensive phone calls.

- Offer to accompany the patient to the doctor and be the one who takes the notes.

- Offer specific assistance in the way of grocery shopping, meals, errands, and transportation to physician appointments, physical therapy, or the pharmacy.

> ☞ Give the patient a call before you leave for the grocery store, the mall, or the pharmacy; let them know where you are going and volunteer to pick up something for them. Ask before you set out if they will call ahead and pre-charge or whether they will reimburse you.

- Call at a time when you know the answering machine will pick up and leave a message that you are thinking of them and not expecting a return call.

- Suggest that the pharmacist at the patient's pharmacy be advised about the illness and potential patient needs.

- Inquire if there are special needs such as a hospital bed, plastic mattress cover, or other equipment. Families are often under so much pressure they might gratefully accept your offer to do some comparison pricing, put an item on hold, or do the shopping.

- If the illness and/or convalescence falls during a holiday period, offer to contribute to holiday preparations. You can bake and decorate Hanukkah or Christmas cookies, prepare Easter baskets, cook a pot of chicken soup and matzo balls, wrap holiday presents, or select and address greeting cards. Bringing the holiday spirit to someone who is ill will surely bolster their spirits.

- Encourage the person to speak.

- Be an active listener.

- Think carefully before you speak.

- Give your full and undivided attention when listening to them.

- Restrict conversations to short periods so you don't tire the patient.

- Choose words and actions that express compassion.

- Be careful in offering advice, even if you are asked; they are the ones who will live with the consequences of the decisions they make.

- Reassure them that whatever they are feeling is normal.

- Encourage them to share their feelings when they are ready.

- Recommend they explore support groups. Many people find it comforting to interact with others who are experiencing the same problems, and they can be especially helpful if they are feeling isolated. Support groups can be found in diverse settings; some hold meetings, and others are online discussions or forums.

> ☞ If you would like to buy or loan a book on tape or CD, make sure they have a player (and batteries) so they can listen.

- If someone is well enough to read, send them a book to read rather than recommending one.

HOW TO SAY IT

Are you up to a visit?

Can I take the children to a movie?

How are you doing with all of this?

I am here for you.

I am here to listen.

I am on my way to the grocery store; what can I pick up for you?

I am thinking of you.

I am willing to help in any way I can. (Ensure that you follow through.)

I have a free hour tomorrow afternoon. I can run an errand for you or do some of your housekeeping—your choice.

I will be at the pharmacy this afternoon; let me know if there is something you need that I can pick up.

It is so good to see you.

It must be difficult to go through this.

Let me take care of that for you.

What can I do to help you?

Would you like some company?

WHAT NOT TO SAY AND DO

- Don't change the subject or end the conversation if they are frightened. If they tell you "I'm afraid," you can ask them "What are you afraid of?" Or you can ask them "Is there anything I can do to make you less frightened?" or "Is there anyone I can talk to to help minimize your fear? Your doctor? Your clergy?"

- Don't excuse yourself if they are angry and need to vent. Anger is part of the grief and healing process, and they need to release their feelings.

- Don't use a statement that minimizes the situation, such as "You are lucky that . . ."

- Don't compare their experience or the way they are coping to another person's, such as "My co-worker didn't miss a beat and was back to work after a week."

- Don't find something good in it, such as "If you had to get (a disease), this is a good one to get."

- Don't deliver unrealistic or false assurances, such as "You'll be as good as new."

- Avoid statements that imply they are responsible for their problems, such as "I wish you hadn't . . ."

- Don't tell them "You don't deserve this." Realistically, who does? But it is okay to empathize with their possible feelings, such as "This is *so* unfair!"

- Avoid any message that expresses pity or increases a person's sense of helplessness or victimization, such as "I wouldn't wish this on my worst enemy."

- Don't interrupt. Avoid any conversation or thoughts, no matter how important you think they are, that break their train of thought or speech.

- Avoid messages that infer that it is "God's will" or they somehow deserve what has happened.

- Don't use sentences that begin with "You should," as it appears as if you are imposing your views, opinions, or advice.

- Don't share pessimistic opinions, such as "He won't live long."

HOW NOT TO SAY IT

At least it isn't life-threatening.

Being so sad isn't going to help you recover.

Don't be scared.

Don't worry.

I'm sure everything will be okay.

It says in the book you gave me that you can live a normal life.

Lying around isn't going to make it better.

The diagnosis could have been a lot worse.

This is so sad. Let's talk about something positive.

You shouldn't be angry.

You shouldn't be sad.

You're being a worrywart.

NONVERBAL STRATEGIES

Beyond being supportive through words, your help can come in the form of action. Each of us has an expertise, one thing that seems to come easier than anything else and that we are always good at. You might have a recipe for a soup that is your signature dish—one that you always prepare or keep in the freezer in case someone is in need. Well, now someone is. Offer to bring some over. Or you might be a whiz on the Internet, always locating information and resources that seem to elude others. See if you can help out with some online searching.

Take a look at the following list of ideas and helpful actions. Don't be overly ambitious and promise what you can't deliver. You can offer to help in any of these ways, but realize that someone might already have chosen their physician, surgeon, or course of action. If your initial offer is refused, choose something else and offer again.

- Conduct research on medical tests and potential treatments.

- Conduct research on specialists and surgeons who have an expertise in the illness or problem.

- Conduct a search for current and future clinical trials.

- Search for medical facilities that have an expertise in the illness, problem, or procedure.

- Conduct research on surgical options.

- Investigate pharmaceuticals and holistic treatment options.

- Conduct a search for medical literature.

- Identify appropriate support groups and include information on when and where they meet.

- Offer to act as an advocate.

- Offer housekeeping help in the way of vacuuming, dusting, food shopping, or laundry.

- Provide needed transportation, whether it is for physician appointments, children's carpools, or after-school activities.

- Volunteer to watch the children or keep the children at your home.

- Offer to prepare meals or organize neighbors or friends to sign up to deliver meals.

- If you are skilled in organization or bookkeeping, offer to track, reconcile, and organize health insurance invoices and bills.

Special Situations

A relative called with the news that a cousin has been diagnosed with a chronic illness, and I have never heard of it. I have no idea what to do or say.
It's okay to do nothing for a few days until you learn more about the illness and the diagnosis. It would be helpful to do a little research to understand the illness, symptoms, and treatment options—not to give your cousin advice but so you can listen and better understand your cousin's situation. Begin online or at your public library. Once you are familiar with the illness, either write your cousin a note and express your concern or give them a call. We expect more from our families, so be sure to make some contact, even a greeting card that says you're thinking of them.

An acquaintance called to tell me they heard my co-worker was in a car accident while on vacation and is in bad shape. The co-worker is in the intensive care unit, and I don't know what to do.

Immediately contact your supervisor and let them know what has happened. There are other ways to support the family, but further interaction might depend on how close you are to the co-worker. You can contact the hospital and get an update on their condition. The hospital can tell you how to reach family members. You can speak with a social worker to learn the seriousness of the injury and get any suggestions on what you or the office can do to help. You can ask for donations from the office and send flowers or arrange meals for the family members. The family might welcome help in researching information or resources or relieving them of some duties you can do from your home location. You can offer to notify people. If you are a close friend, you might request permission from the family to join them at the hospital.

A colleague has taken a leave of absence while undergoing chemotherapy. How can I stay in touch and show my support?

It's very isolating changing daily routines and support systems while dealing with illness and treatment. You can help your colleague feel less isolated by keeping in touch and helping others in the office do the same. A short note can make a tough day seem less so. Because many people are willing to help but are unsure of what is appropriate, you could circulate a memo that provides your colleague's mailing address and a suggestion that co-workers send cards and notes to keep in touch, too. Meals are often welcome, but some treatments alter taste and impact the digestive system. Ask what foods are welcome and if there are any allergies, restrictions, or preferences. If you are willing to be a co-ordinator, you can initiate a sign-up sheet for others in the office to take a turn and communicate the food requirements. Check with your colleague's supervisor to coordinate any other outreach effort. You could also make a donation to a charitable organization in honor of your colleague and in hope of a speedy recovery. This gesture might bolster your colleague's spirits and make them feel good knowing that your remembrance will also help someone else in need.

A friend's newborn baby is having serious problems and has been transferred to a children's hospital.

Ask your friend if you can visit at the hospital and if so, what would be a convenient time. It might be comforting for you to bring the parent(s) lunch or take them out for lunch. Hospital food can be unappealing, so anything homemade or purchased from a favorite food outlet is always appreciated. Offer to keep them company while the baby is having a procedure or for a set period of time. Bring along a magazine or novel to distract them. Inquire if they need items purchased for themselves or the baby. They might need transportation for friends or relatives arriving from out of town. Let your friend know you'd like to support them in any way you can, and make yourself available if they need to talk or require assistance.

A family member shared that she has a potentially debilitating chronic illness. I did some research and tried to ask her how she is doing, but she shrugs it off and changes the subject. Should I continue to follow up with her or just forget it?
Chronic illnesses are tricky; there are times when someone feels really sick and needs help and other times when things are in control and the individual just wants to be like everyone else and go about their business. It might be that your family member's illness is under control and they would rather not talk about it. Keep in touch and let them know that you think of them often. You might want to be honest and tell them you would like to be there for them but don't know what kind of a role they would like you to play. Let them know that you want to help in any way you can, and they should let you know what would be most helpful.

SAMPLE LETTERS/E-MAILS

> *To a friend recently diagnosed with a serious illness.*

> January X, 2XXX
> Dear Wendy:

> You've been in my thoughts all day. I have been trying to think of something I could say that would help you through this difficult period, but all I could think to tell you is how much I care about you.

> I promise to support you in any decision you make. I will call you in a week so we can talk about your needs and what I can do to help in the days ahead. You are in my heart and prayers.

> Love,
> Nancy

To a friend whose mother had cardiac surgery.

> October X, 2XXX
> Dear Heather:
>
> Dan's been keeping me posted on your mom's recovery. I was so sorry to hear about the surgery but pleased your mom continues to make progress. It's tough to deal with all this away from your support system, but I know it means the world to your mom to have you with her.
>
> I miss you and look forward to your mom's recovery and your return. If there is anything you need done while you're away, I would be happy to help.
>
> Sending all good thoughts your way.
>
> Love,
> Sharon

To a neighbor recovering from surgery.

> April X, 2XXX
> Dear Malcolm:
>
> I've been getting reports from Peter, and it sounds like you are on the mend. He tells me you can even take the stairs each day—what good news!
>
> I think of you every time I pass your house. I will call next week to see when it's convenient to make a short visit.
>
> Get well soon!
> Luke

To an elderly friend or family member who has just returned home after recuperating in a nursing home.

> March X, 2XXX
> Dear Paul and Mary:
>
> It must be wonderful to be home and back to your routine. I often think of you and hope that you are both doing well.
>
> I bet the views from your window with all the snow must be lovely. I enjoy looking at the snow from inside where it is warm and cozy; shoveling it and driving in it are another matter!

The crocuses should be up by now, and I checked my garden journal the other day to see when they normally appear. Not only should the crocuses be up but the primrose, too; right now those beds have about six inches of snow. My garden journal tells me spring is just around the corner. I wonder if anyone told Mother Nature.

Sending warm thoughts your way. Be well.

Love,
Amanda

For further information:

Albom, Mitch. *Tuesdays with Morrie*. New York, NY: Broadway Books, 1997.

Babcock, Elise NeeDell. *When Life Becomes Precious*. New York, NY: Bantam Books, 1997.

Callanan, Maggie, and Patricia Kelley. *Final Gifts: Understanding the Special Awareness, Needs, and Communications of the Dying*. New York, NY: Bantam Books, 1997.

Doka, Kenneth J. *Living with Life-Threatening Illness: A Guide for Patients, Their Families, and Caregivers*. San Francisco, CA: Jossey-Bass, 1998.

Doka, Kenneth J., ed, and Joyce Davidson. *Living with Grief: When Illness Is Prolonged*. Washington, DC: Hospice Foundation of America, 1997.

Kabat-Zinn, Jon. *Full Catastrophe Living: Using the Wisdom of Your Body and Mind to Face Stress, Pain and Illness*. New York, NY: Delta, 1990.

Kane, Jeff, M.D. *Be Sick Well: A Healthy Approach to Chronic Illness*. Oakland, CA: New Harbinger Publications, Inc., 1991.

American Cancer Society
1599 Clifton Road, NE
Atlanta, GA 30329-4251
(800) ACS-2345
www.acscsn.org

American Heart Association
7272 Greenville Avenue

Dallas, TX 75231

(214) 373-6300 or (800) AHA-USA1

www.americanheart.org/presenter.jhtml?identifier = 1200000

American Lung Association

1740 Broadway

New York, NY 10019-4374

(212) 315-8700 or (800) LUNG-USA

www.lungusa.org

American Parkinson Disease Association, Inc.

1250 Hylan Boulevard, Suite 4B

Staten Island, NY 10305-1946

(718) 981-8001 or (800) 223-2732

www.apdaparkinson.org

Hospice Foundation of America

2001 S Street, NW #300

Washington, DC 20009

(800) 854-3402

www.hospicefoundation.org

The Leukemia and Lymphoma Society

1311 Mamaroneck Avenue

White Plains, NY 10605

(914) 949-5213 or (800) 955-4572

Multiple Sclerosis Association of America

706 Haddonfield Road

Cherry Hill, NJ 08002

(800) 833-4672

National Association of People with AIDS

1413 K Street, NW

Washington, DC 20036

(202) 898-0414

www.napwa.org

National Cancer Institute
9000 Rockville Pike, 31 Center Drive
MSC 2580
Bethesda, MD 20892-2580
(301) 496-5583 or (800) 422-6237 or TTY number (800) 332-8615
www.nci.nih.gov

See also: WHAT IS GRIEF? UNDERSTANDING THE PROCESS OF MOURNING AND HOW YOU CAN HELP, WHAT CAN I DO? HOW TO LISTEN, WHAT CAN I SAY? COMMUNICATIONS THAT COMFORT, and CAREGIVER RESPONSIBILI-TIES.

FIVE

Death of an Adult

"Some people live in our hearts forever."

—Anonymous

D EATH is a natural and inevitable part of life and something we all have to deal with at some time. Although the cessation of life is a familiar concept, it is impossible to comprehend the permanence of a loved one's death unless you have personally experienced it. None of us can anticipate how we will react to the death of someone we care about or even someone we might not know well. The nature of our relationship—parent, grandparent, sibling, spouse, child, friend, cousin, neighbor, or co-worker—and the circumstances of the death both play a part in our personal response.

The finality of death brings on a tremendous sense of loss. The deep feelings of sorrow caused by the loss are expressed in grief, and this period is called be-reavement. Mourning is the painful process of working through the grief, and it is through this process that we learn to live with our loss.

Grieving is not like any other experience. No matter how often you do it, you never get better at it, and even if you have done it before, it doesn't make the process any easier. You never get used to grieving, and the process can and is dif-ferent with each death you experience because every relationship is different.

Most of us relish our routines and personal rituals because they bring order and pleasure into our daily lives. Death triggers personal chaos, and the ordered world the bereaved lived in no longer exists. Many find that participation in tra-ditional mourning observances restores some order to the chaos and brings a spiritual and emotional strength.

Mourners should be encouraged to express their grief. Held inside, grief will fester over time, eventually surfacing in destructive ways. Grief does not go away on its own.

Much has been written about the stages of grief (see Chapter One), described as periods of denial, anger, guilt, bargaining with God, depression, and acceptance. But grief manifests itself in many emotions that make it hard for others to interact with the bereaved. Some of the stages can be strange, very strong, and frightening.

Many books provide guidelines for the stages of grief along with timetables predicting the duration of the stages. It must be remembered that these truly are guidelines. Individuals grieve in their own way, and stages can last anywhere from one day to weeks or months. It might take the bereaved one to several years to fully accept their loss.

If you are like many folks, you might fear death and have yet to come to terms with your own mortality; don't let this fear keep you away from the bereaved. Death and bereavement are not contagious, and the experience of grief and mourning won't make you more susceptible to it. Your care and concern, expressed through verbal, nonverbal, and written communications, makes you an essential link in the healing process.

THINGS TO CONSIDER

- The circumstances of death, whether unexpected, from a long illness, or an accident.

- The nature of your relationship with the deceased.

- The personal requests of the family.

- The religious or cultural beliefs of the bereaved.

- The customs, rituals, or words of comfort in the faith tradition of the bereaved.

- Death changes the identity of the bereaved; they are no longer a husband, wife, partner, mother, father, sister, brother, daughter, or son.

- The bereaved must redefine their role, priorities, and place in a world that is quite different since their loss.

EMOTIONS AND FEELINGS TO ANTICIPATE

- Anger
- Depression
- Disorientation
- Fear
- Forgetfulness
- Guilt
- Isolation

- Loneliness
- Overwhelmed
- Panic
- Rage
- Relief
- Sadness
- Sense of futility

WHAT TO SAY AND DO

- Accept that you are an integral part of the grieving process. Mourners must have a strong support network to cope with the death of a loved one.

- If you are close to the bereaved, there are some difficult tasks that someone should not do alone. You can offer to notify other people, accompany the bereaved to the funeral home, help them choose the casket, or order/arrange food for the post-funeral reception.

- Do make sure the family's religious leader and congregation are aware of the death; the congregation often has resources in place to provide bereavement support.

> ꙮ You might be needed for the short term, but you might also be needed for the long term in handling carpools or child care.

- If there are children among the bereaved, offer concrete ways to help. They might need to shop for appropriate funeral attire, make arrangements for school absence, or pick up homework assignments. Try to anticipate ordinary activities that need to be handled, such as carpools.

- Offer to provide transportation for family or friends coming in from out of town.

- Offer to stay at the house and answer the phone.

- Keep a record of who called, what has been delivered, and by whom.

> ✏ Think of concrete and specific ways to help.

- Volunteer to stay in the house while the bereaved is running errands, attending responsibilities at the funeral home or house of worship, or during the funeral or memorial service.

- Offer to bring over a large-capacity coffeemaker, a large can of coffee, and perishable food necessities.

- Share in the traditional funeral and mourning observances of the bereaved.

> ✏ The bereaved family of a co-worker might not be up to facing the crowds at the office, but there are ways co-workers can help. Offer to sort office belongings into boxes labeled personal and business-related. If the bereaved is uncomfortable coming to the office, suggest a co-worker deliver the boxes. Recommend that a human resources staff member visit the bereaved at home and review benefits paperwork that require a signature.

- Offer to help with correspondence. The task might be less painful if you organize a small group to write and address notes together.

- Allow the bereaved to talk about the deceased as often or for as long as they would like.

- Encourage the bereaved to face and express their feelings.

- Provide an outlet for the bereaved to voice their feelings.

- Offer a shoulder to cry on.

- Cry with the bereaved.

- Share your special memories of the deceased.

- Make a quick phone call just to say hello and let them know you are thinking of them.

- Call on the spur of the moment and invite the bereaved out; you can say "I've made dinner—nothing fancy—won't you please join me?" or "We are going out to get a casual dinner in about an hour; can we pick you up?"

- Offer transportation for a social outing; they might be uncomfortable driving by themselves, especially at night.

■ Be there for the duration. Most folks feel they are most needed for the funeral and immediately thereafter, but you are needed from the first two weeks onward.

■ As the months pass by, so do calls and invitations. They will really appreciate a call and an invitation for lunch.

HOW TO SAY IT

Could you use some help with your correspondence?

Do you want to talk about it?

How are you doing with all this?

I am glad to see you.

I am so sorry for your loss.

I have some free time on Sunday. Why don't I come over, and you can give me your grocery shopping list.

I think of you often.

I will miss (Mary) very much.

Thank you for sharing your feelings with me.

This must be terribly difficult.

What can I do for you?

Why don't I come over and we can make a list of what needs to be done.

WHAT NOT TO SAY AND DO

■ Don't avoid the bereaved. Silence can be isolating and will only add to their pain.

■ Don't tell the bereaved not to cry. Mourners need to cry and express their anger as part of the grieving process.

- Don't think talking about the deceased will be upsetting to the bereaved; they will need to talk about their loss again and again as part of their grieving.

- Don't compare someone's loss to anyone else's—each person's grief is unique.

- Don't judge them. Each person grieves in their own way and in their own time.

- Don't offer quick solutions.

- Don't compare the death of a loved one to your divorce or your pet's death. Even if you have the best intentions and are trying to demonstrate your personal experience with loss, you can't equate your situation to anyone else's.

> ✍ **Don't be alarmed or angered if the bereaved behave in peculiar ways. They are not being disrespectful but absorbing and processing the loss. They will grieve in a way that is appropriate for them and in their own time.**

- Don't assume the bereaved is okay because they have transitioned back into their familiar roles and daily activities. They still need your support.

- Don't show up as a guest, even if you are a family member, without an invitation.

- Don't expect to be entertained when you visit. It would be appropriate to bring something to eat; their bodies as well as their souls need some nurturing.

HOW NOT TO SAY IT

Death is a part of life.

Death was a blessing.

Give me a call if you need anything.

He (she) is in a better place.

He (she) led a full life.

I know how you feel.

I understand how you feel.

If there's anything I can do, just let me know.

It was God's will.

It's part of God's plan.

Keep a stiff upper lip.

Oh, you poor thing.

Something good comes out of everything.

Spare me the details.

Was it expected?

Were they ill?

You look great.

RELIGIOUS AND CULTURAL DIFFERENCES

Funeral and mourning customs are influenced by cultural and religious rituals. It is helpful to understand how different religions and cultures mourn and cope with loss prior to interacting with the bereaved.

It is often appropriate to bring food, and you'll find this information under the following "What to Bring" section. It is important to ask first if the family observes special dietary laws or if there are special dietary needs based on food allergies.

Respect the family's wishes, particularly regarding flowers. Flowers are not sent at all in some faiths, and some families prefer their loved one be remembered with a donation rather than flowers.

The following guidelines provide basic information on how different religions deal with death and mourning. This section will help you understand what to expect, but since there are many different branches, sects, and denominations, it is important that you personally check with the funeral home, religious institution, or bereaved family to clarify their preferences.

BUDDHIST

What to Expect

- There are different sects of Buddhism, and their traditions for memorial services vary. They all share a great respect for the dignity and eternity of each human life.

- There is no one prescribed order of funeral services for all Buddhist sects. Funeral services can be held at a funeral home, the home of the bereaved, a community center or at a temple.

- A post-memorial service might be held ninety days after the death.

- Close family members and friends observe the first anniversary of death, and subsequent anniversaries are observed in private.

What to Wear

- Subdued, modest clothing appropriate for funerals; you should inquire, as dark dress is appropriate for some sects and light dress for others.

- Call ahead for seating details if the service is held in a temple. You might be sitting on meditation (floor) cushions and need to dress appropriately.

What to Do

- Pay respects to the family prior to the start of the funeral service.

- View the body, bowing slightly.

- Make a charitable donation if the family chooses a charity or cause in memory of the deceased.

What to Bring

- Send flowers to the funeral.

- Check first to see if food gifts are appropriate; if so, bring a vegetarian dish.

What Not to Do, Say, or Bring

- Avoid wearing the color red.

CHINESE

What to Expect

- Chinese funerals can be made up of a combination of Christian, Buddhist, Confucian, and Taoist rituals, depending on the family's beliefs.

What to Wear

- Modest and conservative dress.

What to Do

- Attend and stay for the entire service. It might be long—up to two hours in duration.

- Walk around the coffin for a final viewing after the service.

- If given a small packet of candy and a red lucky money envelope at the funeral, eat the candy immediately and spend the money on a small treat.

- Turn away as the coffin is lowered into the grave, as it is considered unlucky and impolite to watch.

- Attend the funeral meal after the burial.

- Visit the family during the month of mourning.

What to Bring

- Flowers in colors of white or yellow only. Chrysanthemums are very popular.

- Gifts of food when visiting the family during the mourning period.

What Not to Do, Say, or Bring

- Do not bring flowers with thorns, especially roses in any color.

HINDU

What to Expect

- Hindus believe in reincarnation and cremation, and the funeral service is both a celebration and a remembrance. The funeral ritual frequently includes noise, usually horns and bells, and flowers and sweetmeats might be passed around as offerings.

■ The eldest male or the oldest son in the family is the chief mourner and will represent the family in saying good-bye. Male family members might shave their heads to show their respect.

■ The family gathers for a meal and prayers afterward.

■ The mourning period might last ten to thirty days, the family might observe "shraddha"—an eleven-day ritual that liberates the soul so it can descend to heaven.

What to Wear
■ White is a traditional mourning color, but funeral attendees should inquire what is appropriate attire.

What to Do
■ Visit the bereaved at home.

What to Bring
■ Visitors should check before bringing anything when making a post-funeral visit.

What Not to Do, Say, or Bring
■ Do not bring food.

ISLAMIC

What to Expect
■ Muslims believe the soul departs at the moment of death, and immediate burial usually takes place, often within twenty-four hours.

■ Funerals are simple and respectful, and cremation is forbidden.

■ Official mourning period is three days but might be longer for a remaining spouse.

■ There might be a special meal to remember the deceased.

What to Wear

■ Dark and modest dress; women should wear a dress and cover their heads and the lengths of their arms.

What to Do

■ Usually only men attend the burial.

What to Bring

■ Baked goods, fruits, or simple meals.

What Not to Do, Say, or Bring

■ Do not send flowers to the funeral.

■ Shoes are not permitted if the service is held in a mosque.

JAPANESE

What to Expect

■ Japanese traditions are a blend of Buddhist and Shinto influences.

■ The family might observe Shojingyo, a forty-nine-day period of mourning, or they might observe a longer period, depending on their religious beliefs.

What to Wear

■ Simple and conservative black clothing; dark blue is acceptable. No one should wear shiny black shoes, and women should wear dark tights.

■ Women should refrain from wearing jewelry; a strand of pearls is acceptable, as it resembles a tear.

What to Do

■ Attend the funeral.

■ Be prompt.

■ There should be a table set up at the entrance with someone to greet visitors. Sign your name in the registry, and present a monetary gift called "koden" to defray the funeral costs.

■ Put crisp, new bills in a clean, new, white envelope (a supply of envelopes may be available at the funeral home or can be purchased at Japanese bookstores). Traditionally, if you could not get brand-new bills, the bills were ironed. This is no longer required if you do not have the time.

■ You may write a check, but it does not convey the same courtesy as cash bills.

■ If you pay a condolence visit and a salt shaker is provided prior to entering the home, sprinkle salt on yourself outside the home to purify yourself before entering the house.

What to Bring

■ Flowers in shades of white and yellow, white being the most desirable; chrysanthemums are most frequently given, as they are an important flower and represent the emperor.

What Not to Do, Say, or Bring

■ Do not wear red to the funeral or give red flowers, as red represents blood.

■ Do not give flowers with thorns.

■ Do not give money gifts in increments of four or containing four because the pronunciation of the word *four* is the same as the word for death.

JEWISH

What to Expect

■ The burial must take place as soon as possible—within twenty-four hours after death but no more than two days after the death. Burial may be delayed if the immediate family must travel long distances.

■ Funerals are not held on the Sabbath, Rosh Hashanah, Yom Kippur, Festival of Tabernacles (Sukkot), Passover (Pesach), and Feast of Weeks (Shavuot).

■ There is no wake.

■ There is no viewing; the casket remains closed.

- Mourners may have a symbolic small tear—keriah—made to their clothes, which represents a broken heart.

- Family observes shiva for seven days—the Hebrew word for *seven* is "shevah," and *shiva* is taken from *shevah* to mean there are seven days of mourning after the funeral.

- Family continues to observe mourning during sh'loshim (Hebrew for thirty) for twenty-one days, the three weeks following shiva. The family returns to work but does not usually attend social functions.

- Families observe yahrtzeit, the annual anniversary of a loved one's death.

What to Wear
- Dark and conservative clothing.

What to Do
- Family members and friends, regardless of their religion, gather at the home to comfort the mourners during shiva. Visitors are not expected to cheer up the mourners—they should follow the lead of the mourners and be either silent or listen to the mourners speak of the deceased.

- It is appropriate to make charitable contributions in memory of the deceased.

- Visits from friends are especially appreciated during Sh'loshim, as condolence visits have usually slowed down and mourners might feel especially isolated.

What to Bring
- It is customary to provide food to the mourners during the shiva week.

- Bring baked goods, fruit, or meals (without pork or pork products) that need only to be reheated.

What Not to Do, Say, or Bring
- Do not send flowers, as all aspects of the funeral are to be as simple as possible.

PROTESTANT

What to Expect

- Some Protestant denominations have established rituals which would include three parts of the funeral service—the visitation, church service, and graveside service. Other denominations are less structured. The family usually notifies you of their plans and expectations through a published death notice in the local newspaper.

- Death notices usually indicate visitation hours and the family's request for flowers or donations. If a notice is not published you can check with the funeral home.

What to Wear

- Dress in a respectful manner, usually in dark colors.

What to Do

- Pay your respects to the deceased at the visitation. Approach the casket or urn, either say a brief prayer or observe a moment of silence, and offer your condolences to the family.

- Sign the guest register at the funeral home.

- Make a charitable donation in memory of the deceased; check the funeral notice for the family's preference.

What to Bring

- Many families prefer that flowers be sent to the funeral home before the funeral or to the church, unless otherwise indicated.

What Not to Do, Say, or Bring

- You are not expected to attend all three parts of the funeral service—the visitation, church service, and graveside service—unless you are a very good friend or family member.

- Do not wear red or bright-colored clothing.

ROMAN CATHOLIC

What to Expect

- There might be three distinct parts to the funeral service—the visitation, funeral mass, and graveside service.

What to Wear

- Black, brown, or dark blue colors are appropriate; jacket and tie for men and dress, suit, or skirt and blouse for women.

What to Do

- Pay your respects to the deceased at the visitation. Approach the casket or urn, either say a brief prayer or observe a moment of silence, and offer your condolences to the family.

- Sign the guest register at the funeral home.

- Make a donation in memory of the deceased; check the funeral notice for the family's preference.

- Visit the family at home.

What to Bring

- Flowers may be sent to the home before or after the funeral or to the funeral home.

- Send a mass card. Contact the Catholic Church office, either a local parish or the parish of the deceased. The office assistant will explain how to obtain mass cards at the parish.

- Send food to the home of the bereaved.

What Not to Do, Say, or Bring

- You are not expected to attend all three parts of the funeral service—the visitation, funeral mass, and graveside service—unless you are a very good friend or family member.

- Do not participate in the communion wine or wafer unless you are Catholic.

- Do not wear red or bright-colored clothing.

Special Situations

I recently learned that a friend from high school was killed in an accident. It has been more than ten years since I was in touch—is it appropriate to write to his parents?

A letter will bring great comfort to your friend's parents, and it is something they can read over and over again. You may share the story of how you met, a memorable experience from your high school days, and reflections on your friendship. It would be thoughtful if you could make a copy of a photo of your friend or one of the two of you from your high school days. Your letter and any memorabilia will be a wonderful keepsake, something they will greatly appreciate, and will help your friend's parents cope with their loss.

My co-worker's mother just died. He asked our supervisor to let the staff know but requested no one speak to him about it so he wouldn't risk breaking down at the office.

You should honor his request not to speak to him at work about his loss, but there are a number of ways you can let him know that you are sorry for his loss. You can send him a condolence card or a written note. If you can't locate his home address, you can leave it for him on his desk or in his mailbox. You can make a donation in his mother's memory; other co-workers might wish to contribute as well, and you can organize a group. If you don't know what specific charity to donate to, contribute to a local group that helps the community.

I learned a year ago that a friend's wife died. I didn't know what to say, so I said nothing and stayed away. I have been thinking a lot about him recently and would like to reconnect.

It is never too late to get in touch with someone you care about. You could break the ice by sending a plant with a note that says "You are often in my thoughts. I would like to see you and will call soon." Or it might be easier to approach him with a letter or note. Be honest, and tell him you are sorry you have been out of touch. You were upset to hear his wife died and unsure how you could help. You have really missed his friendship and would like to rekindle the relationship. You might invite him to be your guest at lunch, dinner, or a movie. Let him know you will call him in a few days to schedule a date, and follow up with a phone call.

My estranged friend's mother just died.
Let your friend know that you are so sorry for his loss and he has your deepest sympathy. If you would like to open the door to renew the relationship, communicate that you would like to be there for him and are ready to help. If his response is receptive, plan to help him in ways that are comfortable for you.

SAMPLE LETTERS/E-MAILS

To a good friend/colleague whose husband died after five years in an incapacitated state.

> January X, 2XXX
> Dear Elizabeth:
>
> Mark and I were so saddened to hear of Mike's death. I wish there was something we could say or do to ease the pain. Please know how much I value our friendship, your talents, and your support. I would like to be there for you, too. I will keep in touch to see what we can do to make the next few days, weeks, and months easier for you and your family. You, Jared, and Michelle will be in my thoughts and prayers.
>
> Love,
> Nancy

To the mother of your friend on your friend's death.

> September X, 2XXX
> Dear Mrs. Harper:
>
> I was deeply saddened by my dear friend Alexandra's death. Your daughter was a very special friend, and I feel richer for having had the pleasure of knowing her. I will miss her terribly, and I know you will too.
>
> Alexandra and I shared so much. Our lives were so entwined, and I have the most wonderful memories of her.
>
> In the next few months, I plan to look through my albums and gather together photographs of Alexandra's and my adventures. I will give you a call

when I have finished, and I would like to get together with you to share the photographs.

In the meantime, you have my heartfelt condolences.

Sincerely,
Mary Beth

To a cousin on the death of her father.

August X, 2XXX
Dear Sharon:

We are all so sad your dad died, and know that our grief is only a small portion of what you must be feeling.

I just wanted to take a moment and share some thoughts about your dad and what he meant to me. When I think of your dad, the first word that comes to mind is *fun*. From my earliest recollections, your family always seemed to be such an active and involved bunch, and that is always how I think of your dad. I can only imagine what a great teacher he must have been because he had such a keen interest in so many things. It was always interesting to talk to him.

I am so glad our families were able to share their last years together in such close proximity. They had such a rich and shared history, which we are all connected through and to each other. For this, I am most grateful.

I am thankful that I got to spend a whole afternoon with your dad when I was in Florida in April. Your dad was looking pretty well for all the health problems he was having, and we had a good visit.

He was so proud of you, and he had every right to be. What an achievement your dad's life was. He raised all of you after your mom died at a time when it was unusual to have a single-parent household. Whatever difficulties he experienced in life, he overcame and found such joy in his relationships with his children and grandchildren.

We will all miss him—while we didn't see him regularly, we communicated with him often and knew that he was a part of our life and our family. We will remember him with love, humor, and pride.

You are in my thoughts.

Love,
Ellen

To the daughter of a friend on the death of her mother.

October X, 2XXX

Dear Teresa:

It is with great sorrow that I learned of your dear mother's death. Words cannot tell you how much I will miss her and how much she affected my life. I am sure the pain you must now feel is tempered by all the wonderful memories you have of this extraordinary woman. As the years go by, missing her will bring to mind those meaningful times you spent together. You must know how very proud she was of you. Her conversations were always replete with things about her family, her love, and her pride.

Mothers are very special people in our lives, and it is always difficult to lose them, no matter their age or ours.

May you be a living tribute to your mom's memory. Know that I, too, will remember your dear mother with much love and gratitude.

Caroline

To a nephew's wife whose mom died four months ago.

May X, 2XXX

Dear Cindy:

You are often in my thoughts. How are you, Steve, and the children doing? I remember feeling very much alone several months after my mom's death. Everyone I knew was back to their normal routine, and I had a sense that nothing in my life would be normal again. It was a very sad period, and I missed my mother terribly.

It's a difficult time as you adjust to life without your mom. I know you two had a special relationship, and that will always remain. It takes time for the pain and sense of loss to subside, but when it does, it is wonderful to bring those special feelings and warmth back into your life.

I don't have many words of wisdom. I just wanted you to know that you are thought of and cared for. Be kind to yourself, and give Steve and the children a kiss for me.

With love,

Aunt Jenny

A very belated sympathy letter to an acquaintance on the death of her husband.

June X, 2XXX

Dear Teresa:

Please accept my apology for taking so long to write this note. I was so sorry to hear of John's death last August. We frequently mentioned him in our prayers at services and hoped the treatments he was receiving would work.

We really enjoyed getting to know John through the religious school programs, and his warmth and friendliness made many of the meetings a much more pleasant experience.

What always struck me about John was his smile and his interest in the people around him. His sincerity and easygoing nature made the day brighter. He is sorely missed.

Please accept my deepest sympathy on your loss. You are in my heart and prayers.

Sincerely,

Harriet Brown

For further information:

Bartocci, Barbara. *Nobody's Child Anymore: Grieving, Caring and Comforting When Parents Die.* Notre Dame, IN: Sorin Books, 2000.

Commins, Patricia. *Remembering Mother, Finding Myself.* Deerfield Beach, FL: Health Communications, Inc., 1999.

Deits, Bob. *Life After Loss: A Personal Guide to Dealing with Death, Divorce, Job Change and Relocation.* Tucson, AZ: Perseus Publishing, 1999.

Doka, Kenneth J., Ph.D., ed. *Living with Grief After Sudden Loss: Suicide, Homicide, Accident, Heart Attack, Stroke.* Bristol, PA: Taylor and Francis, 1996.

Kübler-Ross, Elisabeth. *On Death and Dying.* New York, NY: Scribner, 1997.

Mathis, Stuart M., and Arthur J. Magida, eds. *How to Be a Perfect Stranger: A Guide to Etiquette in Other People's Religious Ceremonies.* Woodstock, VT: Jewish Lights Publishing, 1996.

Noel, Brook, and Pamela D. Blair, Ph.D. *I Wasn't Ready to Say Good-bye: Surviving, Coping and Healing After the Sudden Death of a Loved One.* Milwaukee, WI: Champion Press Ltd., 2000.

Rando, Therese A., Ph.D. *How to Go on Living When Someone You Love Dies.* New York, NY: Bantam Books, 1991.

American Association of Retired Persons (AARP), Grief and Loss, a collection of resources, a community of care
www.aarp.org/griefandloss

GriefNet.org is an Internet community of persons dealing with grief, death, and major loss with forty-seven e-mail support groups and two websites.
GriefNet.org

Especially for teens:
Fitzgerald, Helen. *The Grieving Teen: A Guide for Teenagers and Their Friends.* New York, NY: Fireside, 2000.

Grollman, Earl A. *Bereaved Children and Teens: A Support Guide for Parents and Professionals.* Boston, MA: Beacon Press, 1996.

————. *Straight Talk About Death for Teenagers: How to Cope with Losing Someone You Love.* Boston, MA: Beacon Press, 1993.

Wolfelt, Alan D., Ph.D. *Healing Your Grieving Heart for Teens.* Fort Collins, CO: Companion Press, 2001.

Especially for children:
Buscaglia, Leo, Ph.D. *The Fall of Freddie the Leaf.* New York, NY: Henry Holt & Company, Inc., 2002.

Coleman, Dr. Paul. *How to Say It to Your Child When Bad Things Happen: Good Answers to Tough Questions.* Paramus, NJ: Prentice Hall Press, 2002.

————. *How to Say It to Your Kids.* Paramus, NJ: Prentice Hall Press, 2000.

Krementz, Jill. *How It Feels When a Parent Dies.* New York, NY: Knopf, 1988.

Mundy, Michaelene. *Sad Isn't Bad: A Good-Grief Guidebook for Kids Dealing with Loss*. St. Meinrad, IA: Abbey Press, 1998.

See also: WHAT IS GRIEF? UNDERSTANDING THE PROCESS OF MOURNING AND HOW YOU CAN HELP, WHAT CAN I SAY? COMMUNICATIONS THAT COMFORT, and WHAT CAN I DO? HOW TO LISTEN.

SIX

Death of a Child

*"The true way to mourn the dead is to take care
of the living who belong to them."*

—Edmund Burke

PARENTS expect to die before their children; when a child dies it is not in the natural order of things, and nothing prepares us for burying and mourning our children. Hopes and dreams for the future die along with the child. Because a child is so intimately linked to its parents, it is easy for the parents to feel as if they have lost a piece of themselves.

Parents report an aching sense of guilt and personal responsibility when children die from accidents, homicide, and suicide, the leading causes of death among young people. They might exert enormous effort replaying and reliving the moments of the day the death occurred, desperately trying to figure out what they could have done differently to prevent the outcome.

The death of a child is deeply unsettling, and because of its infrequency, it is easy for parents to feel very isolated. Parents can feel an enormous emptiness in their homes and in their hearts. It is a loss that is keenly felt by both parents, grandparents, and any surviving children.

Parents describe the grief as so overwhelming that it can bring unique tensions to a marriage. Unlike other losses and disappointments, parents who had previously been able to provide each other with comfort and support might find it difficult to do so when grieving for their child. Each parent might adopt their own coping or grieving approach. These approaches might be neither complementary nor compatible but quite necessary if the parent is to survive the devastating loss.

A parent who experiences the death of a child is forever changed. They don't want to be treated like a victim, and while they yearn to be just like everyone else, this experience has made them different from everyone else. Your job in supporting them in this difficult time is a tough one, but it's absolutely vital.

THINGS TO CONSIDER

- The parent believes that it is his or her role to protect their child, and through no fault of their own, they were unable to do so. They might feel an overwhelming sense of guilt and responsibility.

- Accept that this experience will irrevocably change the parent(s).

- Parents don't "get over it"; they learn to live with the pain.

- Time does not heal all wounds. It makes coping with the loss easier, but the heart never fully recovers.

- Grief might not just be lengthy, it might be everlasting.

- Birthdays of the child and anniversaries of his or her death are particularly painful.

- Recognize that siblings experience a unique loss when a child dies. Take extra care to ensure that you don't ignore the sibling(s), and in your grief, don't imply only the deceased child mattered. If you have a relationship with the sibling(s), continue to nurture it.

EMOTIONS AND FEELINGS TO ANTICIPATE

- Anger
- Blame
- Confusion
- Denial
- Disbelief
- Envy
- Failure
- Guilt
- Helplessness
- Inadequacy
- Incompetency
- Isolation
- Jealousy
- Powerlessness
- Resentment
- Shock

WHAT TO SAY AND DO

- The death of a child is so shocking that the parents might find it difficult to make the simplest decisions or choices. If you are close to the parents, don't ask what you can do, just step in and help them take care of the basic necessities such as caring for other children and pets, meals, snow removal, lawn care, and other daily needs.

- Offer to make calls to places of employment, colleagues, school, family members, or neighbors.

- Do make sure the family's religious leader and congregation are aware of the death; the congregation often has resources in place to provide bereavement support.

- Convey your compassion by acknowledging the loss.

- When you speak about the child, use the child's name.

- Keep in touch on a regular basis.

- Share your memories of the child.

- Do expect the parent(s) to be changed by their experience.

- Do use a "sixth sense" in monitoring your conversations and interactions. Be sensitive when relating news or an experience of your child because it might touch a sensitive or painful nerve.

- If you are a close family member or friend and are willing to help the parent clean the child's room, offer ahead of time. The parent might not know when they will be ready to do so but may appreciate your availability to lend support and comfort.

- Do invite them for holiday celebrations. They probably don't have the energy to prepare a celebration, and they might not be up to it.

- Offer to accompany them to the cemetery.

- Do send a "thinking of you" card to remember them and their child around the child's birthday and the anniversary of the death.

> ◈ When the parent(s) are ready to socialize, find opportunities to create new memories together because the old ones might be too painful. Suggest a new interest such as taking a cooking class or dance lessons together or attending programs at the museum or through adult education. Try a new sport such as bowling or ice skating—something they never did with you or your family.

- Do understand that it might be difficult for the parents to attend graduations, showers, engagement parties, weddings, and visits from your family; these may all be reminders of experiences they will never have with their child.

- Do realize that you might have to accept whatever the parents can give; if you want to continue your relationship, you will have to do so on their terms. They might be emotionally incapable of participating in many of the social rituals you shared in the past, as the memories might be too painful.

- Continue to share your memories of the child throughout the years after their death. It will make the parents feel good to know that their child's special smile, warm greeting, giving nature, or artistic talent is not forgotten.

HOW TO SAY IT

I am so sorry this has happened.

I really don't know how you are feeling, but I would like to be there for you.

I will always miss her (him).

I will never forget him (her).

I'm sad for you.

Take your time; you will do things when you are ready.

There will always be a special place in my heart for him (her) and you.

We loved her (him), too.

We share your sorrow.

WHAT NOT TO SAY AND DO

- Don't visit without an invitation.

- Don't isolate the parents by not sharing any information about your own family; just be sensitive to their loss when you discuss your news.

- Don't treat them as if they are a martyr by making comments such as "I am so proud of you"; they didn't choose to go through this tragedy.

- Don't try to make life appear normal; it's not. Life will never be the same as they knew it, no matter how much you would like it to be. As the parents redefine their lives, life will take on a new "normal."

- Don't be offended if the parent(s) decline your offer for holidays or dinner at your home. Those events might be reminders of past shared experiences.

- Don't automatically assume or expect the parent(s) to continue lifelong patterns and rituals; they might be too painful.

HOW NOT TO SAY IT

At least you have another child.

Be thankful he (she) wasn't an only child.

Don't you wish it was you instead?

God never gives us more than we can handle.

God only takes the best.

He's (She's) in heaven.

I don't know how you are bearing all this; I could never do it.

It happened for the best.

It was God's will.

It would be worse if it was your husband (wife).

Now you have your very own angel.

You'll have other children.

NONVERBAL STRATEGIES

- Make copies of photos you may have of the child and give them to the parents.

- If you are a family member or close friend, you might want to make a small scrapbook of photos from your collection.

- When holiday invitations are declined, bring the holiday to them. Cook and bake holiday foods and deliver them.

- Is there a special holiday ritual you know brought them pleasure? Do it for them, and bring it to their home to enjoy.

- If you are a teacher or classmate, share a project or schoolwork by the child with the parents.

- All the parents have left are memories; share your special memories by writing them down and presenting them to the parents.

Special Situations

I have a sixteen-year-old daughter, and my close friend's sixteen-year-old son was killed in a car accident. How can I deal with this on an ongoing basis?
Be compassionate and caring to your friend, and reach out to her or him, but don't be surprised if it is just too painful for your friend to resume your friendship. Your daughter is and will continue to be a constant reminder of everything your friend has lost. As your child grows and experiences graduation, prom, and college, your friend's child will forever remain sixteen. If the friendship is important to you, you should make an effort to see him or her in nonfamily situations and focus on sharing the adult facets of your life.

My lifelong friend's teenage daughter just died unexpectedly. We have always shared holidays and special occasions together, even vacations. Now she refuses all my invitations. I am heartbroken, too, and wonder if I must lose my friend as well as her daughter?
This person who has suffered the death of her daughter is now a different person, and the person she is today is not the person she might be in a few years. The loss of a child shakes the very core of a parent's existence, and your holidays

and special occasions are a constant reminder of what was and what your friend will never have again. Accept that it is just too painful for your friend to continue this shared tradition. But it is possible for the two of you to continue your friendship. Don't take your friend's refusal personally; she or he is just protecting themselves. Let them know you are ready to resume a relationship when they are. Suggest that you begin a new routine such as coffee on Saturday mornings or an early morning or afternoon walk. Find new ways to be together that provide you both a fresh start and a new foundation for your relationship. When you build new memories together you will retain your friendship, but it will be a different friendship than your past relationship.

A couple my spouse and I are close with lost their young daughter to cancer. Despite our best efforts, we have seen them very infrequently since the funeral and are not sure if they just need to be alone or if they are sending a message that they want us to back off.

Your friends have a rough road ahead of them, but if you are willing, ride it out with them. Keep in touch, briefly if you must, but let them know that you are thinking of them. Give as much as you can, but don't take it personally if you get nothing back. Grief is exhausting, and it might be impossible for your friends to do anything but grieve. Let your friends know that you are available if they want to talk; be their "safe harbor" through nonjudgmental listening. Remember them in small ways on their birthdays and their daughter's birthday or special holidays. Be a continued presence, and wait for them to be ready to resume a relationship. Be patient.

SAMPLE LETTERS/E-MAILS

To a colleague whose teenage daughter was killed in an accident.

> January X, 2XXX
> Dear Bill:
>
> You have been in my thoughts since I heard the shocking news about Linda. The loss of a child is such a difficult grief to bear, and I am so terribly sorry.
>
> There is really nothing I can say to you except that I share your pain. I didn't know Linda personally, but I remember the family portrait you kept in your office, and I enjoyed your stories of her and all that she accomplished in

her short life. I hope that you and your family will find peace again someday. My thoughts and prayers are with you.

Sincerely,
Jim Smith

To the parents of a young child who died after battling cancer for two years.

November X, 2XXX
Dearest Beth and John:

Kelly's death leaves me speechless and in tears. Our thoughts have been with you and your family during this sad week. Losing a wonderful daughter like Kelly is too painful to imagine.

We have the most wonderful memories of the times we spent together on family outings. Kelly was always the adventurous soul, willing to experience new things with such confidence and pleasure. She was sheer joy to be with, and I will never forget her warmth and charm that went beyond her young years. She had a strength and force that let her live life to the fullest during her terrible struggle. She left a legacy of courage that I will try to use as my model as I face the sad days ahead.

We are thinking of you constantly during this difficult time. May you be blessed with the strength and courage to move ahead.

With much love,
Harriet and Sam Little

To the aunt of a teenager killed in a car accident.

June X, 2XXX
Dear Tina:

There are no words to express the shock and sadness I feel over the tragic death of your dear nephew Marshall.

Children are one of life's greatest gifts. Please let your sister and brother-in-law know that my thoughts and prayers have been and will continue to be with all of you during this difficult time.

Marshall was so outgoing and fun-loving that no one who knew him will ever forget him. Though Marshall's time with us was short, his presence touched many lives. May Marshall's memory forever be a blessing.

So much love is sent your way. I will be in touch.
Marianne White

To a teenage friend's family after the friend's death due to complications after surgery.

September X, 2XXX
Dear Mr. and Mrs. Turner and Will:

I was stunned and saddened to learn of Sara's death. Meg had kept me informed, and we were so happy that the surgery had gone well.

Sara will forever remain a bright and shining star that touched my life. She had the sweetest nature, and her smile is etched in my mind. I truly enjoyed being around Sara and looked forward to spending time with her during her convalescence.

Everyone at school is shocked. It is amazing to see what an impact Sara had on everyone's lives. She was so bright and positive-spirited, she seems to have made an impression even on students who didn't know her or were just acquaintances.

Please know that you are not alone in your sadness and grief. I will always feel blessed to have known her.

I found the enclosed photograph yesterday and thought you might like to have it. The picture was taken in our English class last semester when we dressed up like our favorite character. As you can see, Sara was her beloved Scarlett O'Hara.

Much love,
Erica

From a member of the community to the parents of a local teenager who was killed in a car accident.

March X, 2XXX

Dear Mr. and Mrs. Wilson:

Our family was saddened to learn of your recent tragedy and want you to know that it touched our hearts. We are among the many whom you might not know who mourn your loss with you.

May your memories of this special child be sweet and everlasting. You will continue to be in our thoughts and prayers.

Please accept my deepest sympathy.

Sincerely,

Ms. Sharon Landry

For additional information:

Bernstein, Judith R. *When the Bough Breaks—Forever After the Death of a Son or Daughter*. Kansas City, MO: Andrews McMeel Publishing, 1998.

Doka, Kenneth J., Ph.D., ed. *Living with Grief After Sudden Loss: Suicide, Homicide, Accident, Heart Attack, Stroke*. Bristol, PA: Taylor and Francis, 1996.

Finkbeiner, Ann K. *After the Death of a Child: Living with Loss Through the Years*. Baltimore, MD: The Johns Hopkins University Press, 1998.

McCracken, Anne, and Mary Semel. *A Broken Heart Still Beats—After Your Child Dies*. Center City, MN: Hazelden, 2000.

Mehren, Elizabeth. *After the Darkest Hour the Sun Will Shine Again*. New York, NY: Simon & Schuster, 1997.

Rosof, Barbara D. *The Worst Loss: How Families Heal from the Death of a Child*. New York, NY: Henry Holt and Company, Inc., 1994.

Sanders, Catherine M., Ph.D. *How to Survive the Loss of a Child*. Roseville, CA: Prima Publishing, 1998.

Schiff, Harriett Sarnoff. *The Bereaved Parent*. New York, NY: Penguin Books, 1977.

The Compassionate Friends, Inc.

National Headquarters

P.O. Box 3696

Oak Brook, IL 60522-3696
(630) 990-0010 or (877) 969-0010
www.compassionatefriends.org

GriefNet.org is an Internet community of persons dealing with grief, death, and major loss with forty-seven e-mail support groups and two websites. GriefNet.org

Especially for teens:

Fitzgerald, Helen. *The Grieving Teen: A Guide for Teenagers and Their Friends*. New York, NY: Fireside, 2000.

Grollman, Earl A. *Bereaved Children and Teens: A Support Guide for Parents and Professionals*. Boston, MA: Beacon Press, 1996.

———. *Straight Talk About Death for Teenagers: How to Cope with Losing Someone You Love*. Boston, MA: Beacon Press, 1993.

Wolfelt, Alan D., Ph.D. *Healing Your Grieving Heart for Teens*. Fort Collins, CO: Companion Press, 2001.

Especially for children:

Buscaglia, Leo, Ph.D. *The Fall of Freddie the Leaf*. New York, NY: Henry Holt & Company, Inc., 2002.

Coleman, Dr. Paul. *How to Say It to Your Child When Bad Things Happen: Good Answers to Tough Questions*. Paramus, NJ: Prentice Hall Press, 2002.

———. *How to Say It to Your Kids*. Paramus, NJ: Prentice Hall Press, 2000.

Mundy, Michaelene. *Sad Isn't Bad: A Good-Grief Guidebook for Kids Dealing with Loss*. St. Meinrad, IA: Abbey Press, 1998.

See also: WHAT IS GRIEF? UNDERSTANDING THE PROCESS OF MOURNING AND HOW YOU CAN HELP, WHAT CAN I SAY? COMMUNICATIONS THAT COMFORT, WHAT CAN I DO? HOW TO LISTEN, and DEATH OF AN ADULT.

SEVEN

Birth of a Stillborn or Death of a Newborn Baby

"For some life lasts a short while,
but the memories it holds last forever."

—Laura Swenson

THERE is something particularly tragic when a baby dies before birth or shortly after birth. Moms and dads and extended family members have dreamed, planned, and hoped for the day they would meet the new arrival; they wondered who the baby would look like and what characteristics he or she would inherit. This special time winds up filled with sorrow rather than the much-anticipated joy. The mom and dad come home with empty arms and a heavy heart.

The National Center for Health Statistics, Centers for Disease Control Prevention, reports that out of almost 4 million births in the United States in 2000, about 18,737 babies or infants died in the first month of life and 9,250 additional babies died by twelve months. The death of babies up to twenty-eight days is referred to as neonatal death.

Forty-five percent of all infant deaths in 1999 were linked to three leading causes:

- Congenital malformations

- Disorders related to short gestation and low birth weight

- Sudden Infant Death Syndrome (SIDS)

No one knows what to say or do to comfort moms and dads who have lost a baby. Rituals and procedures that provide spiritual and emotional comfort and strength to the bereaved might not exist for stillborns or newborns who live fewer than a full thirty days.

Many adults still turn to their own parents when they need comfort, but it is difficult for the moms and dads to reach out to their own parents for solace when their baby dies because their parents are hurting, too; they have just lost a much-anticipated grandchild and are also bereaved.

Although it might be difficult to comfort someone experiencing such an intensely painful loss, the bereaved will need your prolonged support and help to voice their feelings and fully grieve.

THINGS TO CONSIDER

- Birth defects account for approximately 25 percent of neonatal deaths.

- Premature birth and resulting complications account for approximately 20 percent of neonatal deaths.

- Heart defects account for almost a third of birth-defect-related neonatal deaths.

- Grief and loss are profoundly painful, no matter how old the baby.

- Recognize that siblings experience a unique loss when a fetus or baby dies. Take extra care to ensure that you don't ignore the sibling(s) in your grief. Children are very sensitive to their parents' emotions, so if parents, grandparents, and other adults grieve in a healthy way, the children will learn how to grieve, too.

EMOTIONS AND FEELINGS TO ANTICIPATE

- Anger
- Confusion
- Disappointment
- Disbelief
- Emptiness
- Failure
- Fear
- Guilt

- Helplessness
- Incompetence
- Jealousy
- Pain
- Resentment
- Sadness
- Shock
- Sorrow

WHAT TO SAY AND DO

- It's okay if you cry when you hear the news or when you are with the parent(s).

- Do make sure the family's religious leader and congregation are aware of the death; the congregation often has resources in place to provide bereavement support.

> ༄ If you do visit the family, offer to fix a food they love or bring along a favorite treat. Comfort foods can be nurturing, so consider indulging one or both of the parents' fondness for a special candy, ice cream, bagels, donuts, or a deli sandwich. Even if they have no appetite for it right now, it will warm their heart that you remembered them in such a personal way.

- Plan to attend the funeral or memorial service.

- Offer transportation to and from the airport if family members or friends are coming in from out of town.

- Ask the parent(s) if they picked out a name for their baby. If so, refer to the baby by name.

- Offer to help with household tasks like grocery shopping, laundry, or running errands.

- Bring prepared meals and other groceries the family will need.

- Offer to make phone calls to notify people.

> ༄ If you do accompany the mother to the doctor, suggest you go out for coffee or a diversion afterward.

- Offer to write notes to acknowledge kindnesses if the mom and dad are not up to it.

- Send them a gift certificate for a restaurant or take-out food service.

■ The parent(s) might need some household help; an offer to personally help or a gift certificate for a cleaning service will be appreciated. You can always propose this idea as a group or neighborhood endeavor.

> ↶ If you have a baby yourself, do wait until they ask or offer to hold or help with your baby. They are the only ones who know whether it would be painful or not.

■ Offer to accompany the mom to her post-delivery checkup with the obstetrician.

■ Give the mom a gift certificate for a haircut or spa treatment; it won't take away the pain, but she will look and subsequently feel better.

HOW TO SAY IT

Help me know what I can do to help you.

I can't imagine how sad you must feel.

I love you, and I am so sorry this has happened.

I want to help. What can I do for you?

Is there anything I can do for you?

This must be terribly difficult.

What can I do to help you?

What is your baby's name?

WHAT NOT TO SAY AND DO

■ Don't visit without an invitation.

■ Don't insist on visiting if the mom and dad tell you they are not up to visitors.

■ Don't expect the parent(s) to entertain you. If you are served something, take the initiative to clean up the kitchen before you leave.

- Don't bring your children without checking first.

- If your children accompany you, bring something to keep them occupied and feed them first so they won't be hungry.

- If you have a baby, don't hide the baby from the parents. But don't hand your baby to them to hold; it might be too painful.

- Don't suggest that giving of themselves would make them feel better, for example, donating some of their maternity clothing to someone you know who is pregnant and needy or giving some of the baby clothing and accessories to a needy family.

HOW NOT TO SAY IT

At least you have other children.

At least your baby didn't suffer long.

Don't be so sad.

God doesn't give you more than you can handle.

I hope you didn't hold him (her).

It was better the baby died before you got to know her (him).

It wasn't meant to be.

It's a blessing in disguise.

It's God's will.

There's a reason for everything.

You can have more children.

You're still young.

NONVERBAL STRATEGIES

- If the mom is taking some time off, offer to bring her lunch and share a meal with her.

- If the baby died as an infant, give a baby book as a gift so they can include photos and memories of the baby.

- If they are not up to filling in a baby book, ask them if they would like you to do it for them.

- Save a copy of the local newspaper for them to commemorate and remember the day the baby was born.

Special Situations

A cousin was pregnant with twins. Just before delivery, one baby died; she gave birth to a stillborn and a healthy baby. How do I commemorate this happy-yet-sad occasion?

Although the birth of a child is a joyous event, the parents of these twins have entered a time of great sorrow mixed with great joy. It would be a mistake to assume that the healthy child makes up for the loss of the other twin. The parents lovingly awaited the birth of the two babies, and they will have to mourn the baby who died. It is important to address both the death and the birth separately; if you were to address them together, you would not be recognizing the great sadness and loss for the baby who did not live. You can send a sympathy note for the baby who died, and it would be appropriate to make a donation in memory of the child. You can check with a family member or their religious organization to learn if there is an organization or charity designated for this purpose. You should also send a congratulations, separately, for the healthy baby in whatever way you planned—either by card, flowers, and/or a gift.

A friend had an uneventful pregnancy, but at thirty-two weeks, the baby died and she was induced to deliver a stillborn baby.

It is very important that you acknowledge the baby's death—you will compound her loss if you stay away or never mention that it happened. If your friend chose a name for the baby, it is appropriate to refer to the baby by name. You can send a card, note, or flowers expressing your sympathy. Take your cues from your friend as far as a visit goes; if you do visit with her, give her and her partner a hug, keep them company if they cry, and make yourself available to listen.

SAMPLE LETTERS/E-MAILS

To a friend's daughter and son-in-law whose baby was stillborn.

> July X, 2XXX
> Dear Hillary and Tom:
>
> We were so saddened to hear that your sweet baby daughter died. Words can't possibly express the sorrow we feel for your loss. I know how much you loved your daughter and anticipated her birth.
> I hope that you will find some comfort in knowing that your loss is shared by so many who love you. Please accept our deepest sympathy.
>
> Fondly,
> Steve and Melissa Smith

To friends whose baby died from a congenital problem at three weeks old.

> September X, 2XXX
> Dear Nan and Max:
>
> I was so terribly sorry to hear that Megan died. It was such a joy to share the excitement of her anticipated birth, and I know just how much you treasured her.
> You have been in my thoughts constantly in the last few days. I pray that you will find solace and comfort in your memories of this special child. May these memories be sweet and everlasting.
>
> With love,
> Shannon

To a distant cousin who has had a stillborn baby.

> April X, 2XXX
> Dear Natalie:
>
> Jackie called this morning with the news of your son's birth, and I was terribly saddened to hear that he had died. I have felt so close to you during this pregnancy and share your sorrow.

While I haven't had your experience, I suspect that I know very much how you are feeling. You see, I also lost a baby in infancy.

I've only known you a short time, Natalie, and learned of your pregnancy early in our relationship. I didn't share this with you earlier because I didn't want to frighten you with my story.

You are such a gifted and special person, Natalie. I want nothing more for you and your family than all the goodness you deserve. Let this experience bind you and Aaron closer together. Lean on each other, because no one else knows quite what you are experiencing.

I send much love to you. If you want to share any thoughts with me, please do. I will always be there for you.

Love,
Linda

To a friend on the death of her two-month-old daughter from SIDS.

July X, 2XXX
Dearest Ann:

How does one express such sorrow? You waited so long for Jamie to come into your life. I feel so terribly sad, and I am sorry that you must be asked to endure such grief.

I send my love and support on the loss of your sweet Jamie. The beauty of this child will be locked in your hearts forever.

I will keep you, Jamie, and your dear husband in my prayers.

With love,
Madeline

For further information:

Davis, Deborah L., Ph.D. *Empty Cradle, Broken Heart: Surviving the Death of Your Baby.* Golden, CO: Fulcrum Publishing, 1996.

Douglas, Ann, and John R. Sussman, M.D. *Trying Again: A Guide to Pregnancy After Miscarriage, Stillbirth, and Infant Loss.* Dallas, TX: Taylor Publishing Company, 2000.

Horchler, Joani Nelson, and Robin Rice Morris. *The SIDS Survival Guide: Information and Comfort for Grieving Family and Friends and Professionals Who Seek to Help Them.* Hyattsville, MD: SIDS Educational Services, 1994.

Kohn, Ingrid, MSW, and Perry-Lynn Moffitt, with Isabelle A. Wilkins, M.D. *A Silent Sorrow—Pregnancy Loss: Guidance and Support for You and Your Family.* New York, NY: Routledge, 2000.

Lothrop, Hannah. *Help, Comfort and Hope After Losing Your Baby in Pregnancy or the First Year.* Boulder, CO: Perseus Publishing, 1997.

National Sudden Infant Death Syndrome Resource Center (NSRC)
2070 Chain Bridge Road, Suite 450
Vienna, VA 22182
Toll Free: (866) 866-7437
(703) 821-8955
Fax: (703) 821-2098
www.sidscenter.org

SHARE is a not-for-profit nondenominational organization providing support to those whose lives are touched by the tragic death of a baby through early pregnancy loss, stillbirth, or newborn death.

National SHARE Office
St. Joseph Health Center
300 First Capitol Drive
St. Charles, MS 63301-2893
(636) 947-6164 or (800) 821-6819
Fax: (636) 947-7486
share@nationalshareoffice.com
www.nationalshareoffice.com

The Compassionate Friends, Inc.
National Headquarters
P.O. Box 3696
Oak Brook, IL 60522-3696
(630) 990-0010 or (877) 969-0010
www.compassionatefriends.org

Especially for children:

Buscaglia, Leo, Ph.D. *The Fall of Freddie the Leaf*. New York, NY: Henry Holt & Company, Inc., 2002.

Coleman, Dr. Paul. *How to Say It to Your Child When Bad Things Happen: Good Answers to Tough Questions*. Paramus, NJ: Prentice Hall Press, 2002.

———. *How to Say It to Your Kids*. Paramus, NJ: Prentice Hall Press, 2000.

See also: WHAT IS GRIEF? UNDERSTANDING THE PROCESS OF MOURNING AND HOW YOU CAN HELP, WHAT CAN I SAY? COMMUNICATIONS THAT COMFORT, WHAT CAN I DO? HOW TO LISTEN, DEATH OF AN ADULT, and DEATH OF A CHILD.

EIGHT

Suicide

*"Do not dwell in the past, do not dream of the future,
concentrate the mind on the present moment."*

—Buddha

Suicide is sudden, unexpected, and traumatic. Even if there is a prior history of attempts, suicide is shocking, and nothing prepares the bereaved for the loss.

The National Center for Health Statistics ranks suicide as the eleventh leading cause of death in the United States. Approximately 30,000 individuals die by suicide each year. Suicide ranks as the third leading cause of death for teens and young adults; more teens and young adults die from suicide than from cancer, heart disease, congenital birth defects, AIDS, chronic lung disease, influenza and pneumonia, and stroke combined.

Although suicide is not that uncommon, it bears a social stigma that makes it different from any other death. The bereaved, sometimes referred to as "suicide grievers," might feel shunned by society. They might also feel ashamed; they might be embarrassed to tell people about the death and how it happened, and it is not uncommon for them to keep the cause of death a secret. If a child commits suicide, the parents might feel that sharing the information will reflect negatively on their parenting skills.

The bereaved might feel a sense of responsibility for their loss—shouldn't they have seen it coming, or couldn't they have done something differently that could have prevented the suicide? It isn't just the people closest to the deceased that feel the burden of responsibility; many acquaintances and friends might think they, too, could have done something differently that would have made a difference.

The bereaved might replay past experiences and conversations, searching for clues or some explanation for the suicide. Guilt is unavoidable; their brain is trying to reconcile how this could have happened.

Spiritual and societal rituals and routines that bring comfort to the bereaved might not be available to those dealing with the aftermath of suicide. Some religions might even consider suicide a sin, and burial might be discreet.

The bereaved who witness the suicide or who find the body might compound their grief and experience post-traumatic stress.

It is quite common for the bereaved to experience social withdrawal, and this can easily make them feel isolated at a time when they desperately need support. You can ease this sense of isolation by reaching out to them through oral, written, and nonverbal communications.

THINGS TO CONSIDER

- Police will initially conduct an investigation to rule out homicide before declaring death a suicide. A crime scene must be maintained to identify and analyze the evidence. You will need to check in at the perimeter of the crime scene and request to be with a loved one before entering the area.

- Suicide carries a negative stigma, and it is very common for the bereaved to experience significant shame.

- You might have some experience dealing with death but little or none with suicide.

- Lack of experience makes some folks uncomfortable and fearful; be careful not to treat suicide grievers differently than you would others who grieve the death of a loved one.

- The bereaved might be distressed over unresolved issues.

- The bereaved might be reluctant to talk about their feelings because of the stigma of suicide.

EMOTIONS AND FEELINGS TO ANTICIPATE

- Anger
- Bewilderment
- Confusion
- Despair

- Disbelief
- Embarrassment
- Fear
- Guilt
- Helplessness
- Rage

- Rejection
- Remorse
- Resentment
- Shame
- Shock

WHAT TO SAY AND DO

- Do make sure the family's religious leader and congregation are aware of the death. The congregation often has resources in place to provide bereavement support.

- Do participate in all mourning rituals—attend the wake, funeral, memorial service, or reception.

> ⌒ The bereaved experience a great deal of guilt, and it can easily be misplaced. If you don't attend the funeral or memorial service, they might think you are avoiding them. Assuage these feelings by sending a card or note to express your condolences if you are unable to attend.

- Give unconditional support. It is very appropriate to let the bereaved know that no matter what they are feeling, it is okay.

- Do bring meals and help out in all the ways you would for anyone who is mourning the death of a loved one. See Chapter Five for ideas, customs, and suggestions.

- Be patient and understanding, and roll with the myriad emotions that can be very intense and long-lasting.

- Do bring comfort to the bereaved by mentioning the name of the person who has died.

- Do share your special memories of the person who has died.

- Be sensitive in discussing the deceased; they might have ended their own life, but that doesn't take away from their good character and the life they led.

- Encourage the bereaved to release their feelings. Troubles that are locked inside will fester.

- Allow the bereaved to tell their story over and over again. This is an experience that they might not get over, but in time, their feelings will stabilize.

- Listen and say nothing. No one expects you to have the answers.

- Do keep in touch, as suicide grievers can feel especially isolated.

- Include the bereaved in invitations to a dinner out, a concert, or a movie, and include a few close family members or friends.

- Help the bereaved reestablish routines. If the bereaved is a member of a book club, bridge club, bowling league, etc., offer to pick them up and encourage them to attend.

- Suggest sharing a walk once or twice a week; exercise goes a long way to reestablishing routines and physical health. They might need some coaxing to get out; you might need to let them know you will stop by on Monday and Wednesday at ten in the morning to pick them up.

- Do remember the bereaved at the anniversary of the suicide and other special holidays and events; your thoughtfulness will lighten the sadness.

HOW TO SAY IT

I am here to listen, not to judge.

I am not going to pretend to know how you feel.

I am not going to suggest how you should respond.

I don't have answers, but I will help in any way you'd like.

I know this is a rough time for you.

I might not have any experience with this, but I want to help you.

If you would like some company, I am here for you anytime.

It's good to see you.

Let's take a walk so you can talk and I can listen.

This must be very painful for you.

Would you like to go to a movie with me?

Would you like to talk?

WHAT NOT TO SAY AND DO

- Don't tell the mourner how they should respond; grieving for someone who has committed suicide is different than any other death.

- Don't express your anger at the deceased for taking their life. That is something you will have to deal with, and it is unfair to burden the bereaved with your angry feelings.

- Don't ask if there was a suicide note.

- Don't ask details of the suicide such as "How did Paula take her life?" The bereaved will need to talk about the experience and tell their story many times, but they need to do that with caring people they are comfortable with. Rather than ask questions about the circumstances, offer to be available to listen whenever the bereaved needs to talk.

- Avoid statements that oversimplify the magnitude of loss, such as "Time heals all wounds."

- Avoid judgmental statements relating to the deceased and the cause of death.

- Don't speculate on the reasons for the suicide.

- Don't pass judgment on the bereaved; the experience of suicide might irrevocably change the bereaved, and you'll need to accept the person they have become.

- Don't criticize.

- Don't refer to the deceased as crazy or insane or their actions as irrational.

- Don't compare the experience of the bereaved to that of another suicide griever; everyone adjusts differently, and no two mourners grieve alike.

- Don't avoid the bereaved; if you cross the street or pretend you don't see them, you will heighten their isolation.

- Don't repeat mean-spirited remarks made about the deceased; you'll hurt the bereaved, and you'll look as bad as the person who made the remarks.

HOW NOT TO SAY IT

How are you feeling?

How did they do it?

It was a terrible accident.

It was such a selfish act.

It's God's will.

Snap out of it, already.

The pain will pass.

There must have been signs that she (he) was depressed.

They were crazy.

They were out of their mind.

Think of what you have to be thankful for.

Time is a great healer.

What happened? You'll feel better if you talk about it.

You are holding up so well.

You must be strong for your other children.

You'll get over it in time.

NONVERBAL STRATEGIES

- Offer to help the bereaved create a scrapbook of photos and memorabilia to honor the deceased.

- If the deceased was a part of your group, for example, co-workers or members of a fraternal, professional, or community organization, you might create a memory book for the bereaved. Ask each member to write a personal note about their experience working with the deceased and their thoughts and feelings about them on a more personal level. Include them in a photo album or scrapbook, and present to the bereaved.

- Make a donation to a charitable organization in the deceased's memory.

- Offer to help plant a shrub or garden in memory of the deceased.

- Provide information on local support groups for suicide grievers.

- If the bereaved is uncomfortable going to a support group meeting alone, arrange for a family member to accompany them or offer to accompany them yourself.

- Locate online support groups for suicide grievers. Go to any search engine (www.google.com or www.alltheweb.com) and enter "suicide grief" for the search. You will find a great deal of information that should provide comfort along with interactive list serves where the bereaved can vent their feelings to individuals with common experiences.

Special Situations

A friend's mother was terminally ill with cancer, and she just died. But I don't think her death was from the illness; I think she took an overdose of pain medication.

The end stages of cancer can be brutally painful, and your friend's family has just gone through a terrible ordeal. It would be inappropriate to question your friend on the circumstances of his mom's death; if he chooses to share that with you, it would be a blessing if you could listen and offer compassion. If he does not choose to share this information with you, accept his silence. It is difficult to cope with a parent's illness and subsequent death, and your friend needs understanding. Extend him the same caring support you would provide for any death. Chapter Five will provide you with details on how to help the bereaved deal with the death of an adult. If you have personal or religious reasons that make you uncomfortable or prevent you from lending support, send a sympathy note that expresses your sadness for your friend's loss.

I bumped into an old friend I haven't seen in years, and she shared that her husband died. Surprised, I inquired, "What from?" She told me he committed suicide. I was so shocked, I mumbled something quickly and left. How do I handle the unexpected news of a suicide?

It is shocking to learn that someone you know has taken their life. The survivor is shocked, too, as well as traumatized by the experience. If you leave suddenly, you are expressing your discomfort, which compounds their sorrow. It's okay to be shocked; you could touch your friend lightly on the arm and tell them how sorry you are to learn about their spouse's death. Ask "How are you doing today?" If you have time and are willing, ask them to join you for a cup of coffee. Let them know you have fond memories of them or the spouse. Mention that you will keep them in your prayers.

SAMPLE LETTERS/E-MAILS

To a former co-worker whose husband has taken his life.

> January X, 2XXX
> Dear Mollie:
>
> My deepest sympathy to you and your children on Anthony's sudden death. What a terrible loss to you and everyone who knew Anthony. I have the most wonderful memories of our annual office picnics at Craggy Lake. Anthony was a charismatic storyteller, and I always looked forward to hearing his tales. Anthony will be greatly missed. I will keep you in my prayers.
>
> With fondness,
> Elizabeth Green

To neighbors whose son took his life.

> May X, 2XXX
> Dear Bob and Sheila:
>
> Thinking of you both at this sad time. Robert was a lovely young man with a generous nature and a quick smile. He will be missed by everyone who had the good fortune to cross his path.
>
> We hope that knowing that our love and thoughts are with you will help you through this difficult time.
>
> Love,
> Beth and Michael

To a friend whose wife took her life.

> June X, 2XXX
> Dear Bill:
>
> I am terribly saddened at Susie's death. Susie had many wonderful qualities, and she will be missed. I just don't know what else to say or do because I have never experienced what you are going through. You and the children are in my thoughts and prayers.
>
> Fondly,
> Philip

To an old friend whose teenage son has taken his life.

> February X, 2XXX
> Dearest Sandy:
>
> Words cannot express the deep sorrow I have felt since learning of Alex's death. Memories of our friendship and all the joy we have shared with the children have filled my heart over the last few days.
>
> I remember Alex as a sensitive and loving child. I regret that distance has kept us from spending more time together in the last few years. He will forever be frozen in my memories as the child I dearly loved.

I am so sorry that you are faced with such sadness. I pray that you and your family find the strength to deal with what has to be one of the most difficult losses to bear.

May love and the beautiful memories sustain you. You are in my thoughts and prayers.

Love,
Stacey

For further information:

Doka, Kenneth J., Ph.D., ed. *Living with Grief After Sudden Loss: Suicide, Homicide, Accident, Heart Attack, Stroke.* Bristol, PA: Taylor and Francis, 1996.

Levy, Naomi. *To Begin Again—The Journey Toward Comfort, Strength, and Faith in Difficult Times.* New York, NY: Ballantine Books, 1998.

Robinson, Rita. *Survivors of Suicide.* Franklin Lakes, NJ: Career Press, 2001.

Ross, E. Betsy. *Life After Suicide: A Ray of Hope for Those Left Behind.* New York, NY: Perseus Publishing, 1997.

Viscott, David. *Finding Your Strength in Difficult Times—A Book of Meditations.* Chicago, IL: Contemporary Books, 1993.

American Foundation for Suicide Prevention
120 Wall Street, 22nd Floor
New York, NY 10005
(212) 363-3500 or (888) 333-AFSP
www.afsp.org/

Survivors of Suicide
An independently owned and operated website, in no way associated with any specific group, organization, or religious affiliation, to help those who have lost a loved one to suicide resolve their grief and pain in their own personal way.
www.survivorsofsuicide.com

Beyond Indigo

A privately held company called Kelasan, Inc., based out of Minnesota, Minnesota. The company provides grief support, products, and services to individuals and companies that assist people who are grieving.

www.death-dying.com

See also: WHAT IS GRIEF? UNDERSTANDING THE PROCESS OF MOURNING AND HOW YOU CAN HELP, WHAT CAN I SAY? COMMUNICATIONS THAT COMFORT, WHAT CAN I DO? HOW TO LISTEN, DEATH OF AN ADULT, and DEATH OF A CHILD.

NINE

Miscarriage

*"Friendship improves happiness, and abates misery,
by doubling our joy, and dividing our grief."*

—Joseph Addison

MEDICAL professionals define a miscarriage as any pregnancy loss that occurs before twenty weeks gestational age, approximately up to the fifth month, with most miscarriages occurring during the first twelve weeks.

Clinically, miscarriage is defined as the premature expulsion of a nonviable fetus from the uterus. Medical professionals might view the miscarriage experience in clinical terms and suggest it really isn't a baby but a "product of conception." But to the parents who hoped and dreamed for this pregnancy, the miscarriage is a death in the family and should be treated as such.

There is often no explanation for a miscarriage; almost 50 percent of miscarriages happen because the fetus has failed to develop normally, and the remaining 50 percent occur for no known reason. And sometimes the baby begins life not inside the womb but forms outside the fallopian tube; this is called an ectopic pregnancy. Ectopic pregnancy must be terminated, as the mother's life is at risk if the fallopian tube ruptures; a surgical procedure takes place in which the embryo and part of the fallopian tube is removed. The mother can get pregnant again if the other fallopian tube is healthy.

Couples can feel very vulnerable—they have experienced a loss that was beyond their control. Because many miscarriages happen so early in the pregnancy, sometimes before anyone is told, family, friends, co-workers, and neighbors might not know the couple is grieving until long after the miscarriage.

Mothers and fathers grieve for the child they never knew and will never know. They might have already selected a name, decorated a room, and filled their hearts with love. They grieve for the loss of their baby and yet, in many religions, there is no custom for burying the fetus and no mourning rituals to bring spiritual comfort.

Women might feel extreme guilt after a miscarriage, thinking they are to blame; they might wonder if they should have done something different or contacted their physician earlier. They might exert great effort searching for clues—if only they can figure out what it was they did or experienced during their pregnancy that caused them to miscarry.

Some women feel as if their own body has betrayed them. It is not uncommon for the mom to feel like a failure because it was her body that was to have nurtured and carried the baby to term. Some grieving moms might think irrational thoughts in their grief; they might see babies everywhere they look and wonder why everyone else was able to complete their pregnancy and she couldn't seem to do it.

Miscarriage is not just an emotional loss; it has physical implications as well. The woman's body has undergone hormonal and physical adjustments; she might experience bleeding, cramping, sleeplessness, fatigue, and lack of appetite. She'll need rest and time to regain her strength and emotional well-being. You can play a pivotal role in restoring her emotional well-being through thoughtful and caring verbal, written, and nonverbal communications.

THINGS TO CONSIDER

- No one is at fault. Many miscarriages happen not because of something the mother did or didn't do.

- The family has experienced a death, and they need time to grieve for their loss.

- The mom and dad might grieve differently, but both will need support to talk through their feelings.

- There might be no mourning or burial rites for fetuses.

EMOTIONS AND FEELINGS TO ANTICIPATE

- Anger
- Emptiness
- Failure
- Fear
- Guilt

- Helplessness
- Hopelessness
- Jealousy
- Sadness
- Self-blame

WHAT TO SAY AND DO

- Acknowledge the loss.

- Do show that you genuinely care.

- Do make yourself available to listen.

- It's appropriate to send a card or note.

- Send a bouquet of flowers with a simple note that says "Thinking of you" or "Sending love your way."

> ✍ The mom has experienced physical and hormonal changes and would appreciate some pampering. Offer to help with meals or child care if there is a child at home, or just request that she tell you what would make her feel better.

- Offer a truly funny movie or a comedy tape to provide them with a distraction and release.

- Make yourself available to drive them or accompany them to a medical procedure or doctor appointment.

- Reassure the parents that the miscarriage was not their fault and they should not blame themselves.

- Encourage them to be patient with themselves and the world around them as they adjust to the loss.

- If the couple has other children, offer to babysit so the couple can have some time to themselves.

- Ask the mom and dad if there is something you can do to help them memorialize the baby.

- If they would like to do something in the baby's memory, suggest you plant a tree together.

- If the mom and dad are having difficulty expressing their grief, you can research and provide them with information on local support groups where they can share their experience with others who know what they are feeling.

HOW TO SAY IT

How is your husband/wife?

I am here for you no matter how you need me.

I am not going to pretend to know how you feel.

I am so sorry you lost your baby.

I am thinking of you during this sad time.

I can't imagine how you must be feeling.

I love you, and I am here for you.

I've had a miscarriage, too; if you ever want to talk, let me know.

This must be so hard for you.

This wasn't your fault.

Why don't we sit down and talk about how you are feeling.

WHAT NOT TO SAY AND DO

- Don't ignore the mom or dad and say nothing at all because you don't know what to say.

- Don't ask questions about the experience; if they choose, they will tell you about it in their own time.

- Don't tell them you know someone who had multiple miscarriages. They might think you are minimizing their loss or they should get used to the experience and pain because there might be more.

- Don't tell them they can try again. Another child will not take away the grief of losing this baby who was already loved and cherished.

- Don't allow your discomfort to keep you away. The absence of friends and loved ones could compound an already painful experience.

- Don't change the subject when they try to talk about their loss or their feelings.

- Don't avoid sharing your good news of a pregnancy or birth.

- Don't visit without an invitation.

- Don't ask anything of them. They need time to heal physically and emotionally.

HOW NOT TO SAY IT

At least you can get pregnant.

At least you have another child.

Don't worry; you'll get pregnant again.

It wasn't meant to be.

It wasn't really a person yet.

It's for the best.

It's nature's way of dealing with a problem.

Nature takes care of its mistakes.

So what does this mean for you?

There was probably something wrong with the baby.

You should be feeling better by now.

You're young; you'll have other children.

Special Situations

My friend has had multiple miscarriages.
Your friend must be feeling terribly sad and frustrated. She probably feels that her body has betrayed her, and she will need your support and willingness to hear her out. Women with multiple miscarriages can still successfully carry a baby through term. Be aware that if she becomes pregnant again and is frightened and panicked, these emotions are normal. She'll need love and understanding, and that's what you, as her friend, can give her.

My friend just miscarried, and I am expecting a baby in a few weeks.
Don't assume your friend who has lost a baby will resent you for having a baby. Take your cues from the person who has had the loss. If you exclude her from baby showers and baby announcements, she might feel even more isolated. You could ask her how involved she would like to be. She might indicate it would be too painful to be close to you right now, but it might give her a lift to be involved and share your happiness.

My friend had a second ectopic pregnancy.
Because ectopics often are removed surgically to preserve the mother's life, there is a risk of infertility on the affected side. Your friend is dealing with issues of loss while going through the process of recovering her health. She is probably frightened that she might never get pregnant again and that if she does, she will not carry a healthy baby through delivery. It will be harder for your friend to have a successful pregnancy but not impossible. Be supportive and let her know you are sad for her. Offer support in helping her through her convalescence. Let her know that you intend to support whatever decision she makes in pursuing her desire to be a mom. She needs a willing listener to vent her frustrations and injustice at the difficulty in carrying a baby to term.

SAMPLE LETTERS/E-MAILS

To a friend who has just miscarried early in her first pregnancy.

> March X, 2XXX
> Dear Jane:
>
> I am so sorry to hear about your loss. This must be such a difficult time for you and John. I will call you in the next week to see what I can do to help. In the meantime, know that you are often in my thoughts.
>
> Love,
> Sandy

To a co-worker who has miscarried.

> June X, 2XXX
> Dear Teresa:
>
> I just learned about your miscarriage, and I wanted to tell you how sorry I am. I can't possibly know how you are feeling, but I know how thrilled you were with your pregnancy and this must be a terrible disappointment. I am looking forward to your return to work. We'll have lunch as soon as you feel like it. Until then, I will keep you in my thoughts and prayers.
>
> Fondly,
> Marie

To a sister-in-law who has a child and has miscarried a second time.

> April X, 2XXX
> Dear Madeline:
>
> Will called last night to tell us you miscarried. I am so sorry this has happened. I know how much the three of you have been looking forward to this baby, and it's a terrible loss. I wish there was something I could do or say to make this easier. John and I love you all and are thinking of you constantly. If you'd like some help and company, we are available this weekend and could

drive down on Saturday. I will call you in a day or so to see what you need. I'm sending hugs to all of you.

Much love,
Lilly

To a colleague who has had an ectopic pregnancy and lost a fallopian tube, which will make it harder for her to get pregnant again.

June X, 2XXX
Dear Liz:

I know how excited you were about your pregnancy, and I am so sorry this has happened. It's a terrible blow and so unexpected. You and Steve are such special people, and I know you will make wonderful parents. Don't lose faith. I will call you soon to see what I can do for you. I am more than willing to help in any way.

I am thinking of you both with love and a hopeful heart.
Marianne

For further information:

Allen, Marie, Ph.D., and Shelly Marks, M.S. *Miscarriage—Women Sharing from the Heart.* New York, NY: John Wiley & Sons, 1993.

Douglas, Ann, and John R. Sussman, M.D. *Trying Again: A Guide to Pregnancy After Miscarriage, Stillbirth, and Infant Loss.* Dallas, TX: Taylor Publishing Company, 2000.

Kohn, Ingrid, M.S.W., and Perry-Lynn Moffitt, with Isabelle A. Wilkins, M.D. *A Silent Sorrow—Pregnancy Loss: Guidance and Support for You and Your Family.* New York, NY: Routledge, 2000.

Lothrop, Hannah. *Help, Comfort and Hope after Losing Your Baby in Pregnancy or the First Year.* Boulder, CO: Perseus Publishing, 1997.

Luebbermann, Mimi. *Coping with Miscarriage: A Simple, Reassuring Guide to Emotional and Physical Healing.* Rocklin, CA: Prima Publishing, 1996.

SHARE is a not-for-profit nondenominational organization providing support to those whose lives are touched by the tragic death of a baby through early pregnancy loss, stillbirth, or newborn death.

National SHARE Office
St. Joseph Health Center
300 First Capitol Drive
St. Charles, MS 63301-2893
(636) 947-6164 or (800) 821-6819
Fax: (636) 947-7486
share@nationalshareoffice.com
www.nationalshareoffice.com

See also: WHAT IS GRIEF? UNDERSTANDING THE PROCESS OF MOURNING AND HOW YOU CAN HELP, WHAT CAN I SAY? COMMUNICATIONS THAT COMFORT, WHAT CAN I DO? HOW TO LISTEN, and DEATH OF A STILLBORN OR NEWBORN BABY.

TEN

Pet Loss

"Animals are such agreeable friends—they ask no questions,
they pass no criticisms."

—George Eliot

Pets fulfill a wide range of physical and emotional needs, and they share a
place in our lives as companions, substitute relatives, protectors, and a means
to express our affection. Pets are good for us; they are a source of pleasure,
unconditional love, acceptance, and comfort. It's been proven that pets play a
positive role in wellness and recovery.

So it should be no surprise that the loss of a pet is a painful experience. And
although pet loss is not the same as human loss, the grieving and mourning pro-
cesses are very similar.

Friends, family members, co-workers, neighbors, and acquaintances who
have lost their pet will most likely experience a period of mourning. They might
feel guilty for feeling so terribly sad, but if they are to heal they must express
their grief and mourn for their pet.

A lack of support compounds the grief of someone who is mourning a loss.
Traditionally, society has generated little sympathy when a pet dies. There have
been no religious or social rituals to comfort the bereaved. Some view pet ceme-
teries and pet funerals as bizarre. Comments such as "She was a sweet dog; will
you get the same kind next time?" would be considered heartless if you were
commenting on human loss.

It's important to understand that the bereaved will grieve, and you can significantly help them by acknowledging their loss rather than minimizing it. Grief
must be expressed if one is to heal; grief that is suppressed hampers physical and
emotional well-being and extends the grieving period.

The actual experience of pet loss can trigger an individual's feelings of grief over previous losses—animal *and* human. Even if you do not have a pet or don't feel the depth of attachment to your pet as the bereaved feels to theirs, it is important to acknowledge the loss and support the mourner during this difficult period. Your support in encouraging the bereaved to express their grief will positively impact their healing.

THINGS TO CONSIDER

- Not all pet owners view their pets in the same light; many owners consider their pets as companions and members of their family. They cultivate a special bond with their beloved pet, and there is a depth of emotion and attachment. Others might view their pet as a special part of their life without the deep, emotional attachment. Gauge your response by what you know of the personal involvement, and take your cues from the pet owners when responding to their loss.

- Is the loss a result of a prolonged illness or natural death?

- Is the death sudden?

- Was the pet euthanized?

- Did the loss occur through someone's negligence or by an accident?

- Was the pet placed in a new home?

EMOTIONS AND FEELINGS TO ANTICIPATE

- Anger
- Depression
- Emptiness
- Guilt
- Helplessness
- Loneliness
- Regret
- Sadness

WHAT TO SAY AND DO

- Allow the pet owner to talk openly about their pet and their feelings of loss.

- Demonstrate interest by asking the owner the circumstances surrounding the pet's death or loss.

> ஐ **If the pet is to be taken to the veterinarian for euthanasia, offer to accompany the owner to the veterinarian.**

- If the pet is lost, offer to help circulate flyers in the area or recommend placement of a notice in the local newspaper.

- Encourage the mourner to share stories and memories about their pet.

- Share your own memories of the pet or your recollections of what the person has told you about their pet.

- Send a condolence card. There are cards specifically created for pet loss, and if you can't locate one, convey your own message in a note.

- Plan on following up in a few weeks or months with a note, e-mail message, or phone call to let them know you are thinking of them.

- Send a donation in memory of their deceased or lost pet to any animal-related organization.

- If you have a photograph of the pet, have a copy made for the bereaved or have it framed.

- Offer to help the bereaved create a photo album or scrapbook in memory of the pet.

HOW TO SAY IT

I am so sorry.

I'll always remember your stories about Buddy.

Lucy was a special dog.

Please accept my deepest sympathies.

What a comfort Sally was to you; she will truly be missed.

What sad news; I am so sorry for your loss.

WHAT NOT TO SAY AND DO

- Don't make fun of the pet owner for feeling so sad.

- Don't minimize the loss.

- Don't change the subject when the bereaved begins to share their feelings of loss.

- Don't tell the bereaved to stop dwelling on their pain and remember their happy memories of their pet. Grief must be expressed if the bereaved is to heal.

- Don't minimize the depth of their loss and pain by telling them it was only a pet.

- Don't tell the owner to get on with their life.

- Don't suggest they replace the pet. They need time to grieve before making a decision to get another pet.

HOW NOT TO SAY IT

Be grateful it wasn't a family member.

Don't be so upset; it was only a pet.

It was only a dog (cat, bird, horse, etc.).

Now, now . . . don't cry.

Time heals all wounds.

You can always get another dog (cat).

Special Situations

My seventeen-year-old friend had to sell her horse to pay for college expenses. You can tell your friend how sorry you are and give her a hug. Or you could send her a note and acknowledge what a difficult choice she had to make. Let her know that her horse was so lucky to have a caring human companion. Remind her that the memories she has will bring her comfort and will stay with her always. If you have memories of her horse, she would appreciate having you share them with her. Close your note by letting her know that you are thinking of her.

My neighbor's dog was aggressively difficult. She tried several dog obedience programs, but they just didn't work. She finally had to have him put to sleep.
It is always difficult to make the decision to put an animal to sleep. Let your neighbor know that she did everything she could to help her dog. Make sure she understands that her dog was lucky that his life ended in such caring hands.

My niece's cat was lost. She posted notices but got no response, and she doesn't know what happened to her cat.
Let your niece know how sorry you are that she has lost her cat. Acknowledge that it must be so difficult not knowing what has happened. Remind her that she has done everything she could possibly do, and if you volunteer to help, she won't feel so alone. Let her know that you hope the cat comes back to her.

Someone left my neighbor's gate open; his dog ran out of his yard and was killed by a passing car.
Make sure your neighbor knows that this could have happened to anyone. Let him know that he was a caring owner and did his best to keep his dog safe. He might appreciate it if you share any stories you have of his dog.

My cousin's dog became sick quite suddenly and died.
Express your shock at the sudden and untimely death of your cousin's dog. Be honest and say that you can only imagine how difficult this is for her to deal with. Share with her any special memories you have of her dog, and let her know that her dog was lucky to have her in his life.

SAMPLE LETTERS/E-MAILS

To a colleague who is a freelance writer specializing in dogs, on the death of her Collie.

> March X, 2XXX
> Dear Megan:
>
> I'm so very sorry to hear that you lost Maggie. What a blow. You've been very much in my thoughts this afternoon, and you have my warmest wishes for strength in your grieving and eventual acceptance and peace.
>
> I think of Maggie quite often—the scene you painted in your June article about her rounding up everyone for dinner always comes back to me when I see a certain Collie every morning on my commute in to work—it trots along so beautifully with its owner and always lifts my spirits.
>
> Take good care of yourself and your family, and again, my wishes for strength and peace.
>
> Sincerely,
> Stephanie

To a young niece on the death of her cat.

> June X, 2XXX
> Dearest Lynne:
>
> Your mom called me last night to tell me the sad news about Patches. I am so sorry, Lynne. Patches was a real sweetie and leaves behind wonderful memories. When I think of Patches, I'll always remember her curled at your feet no matter where you sat. Patches was special, and I know you will miss her.
>
> I'm sending love to you, Lynne. Know that you and Patches are in my thoughts. Please extend my sympathies to your mom and dad, too.
>
> Love,
> Aunt Mollie

To a sister whose dog had a terminal illness and had to be put to sleep.

>   October X, 2XXX
>   Dear Beth:
>
>   I'm so sorry—I had no idea. I can only imagine how difficult this is for you and how much courage it took to do the right thing in not prolonging Bailey's suffering.
>   I really don't know what I can do to help, but if there is something I can do, I hope you will let me know. You're in my thoughts.
>
>   With love,
>   Kathy

For further information:

Anderson, Moira K. *Coping with Sorrow on the Loss of Your Pet.* Loveland, CO: Alpine Publications, 1996.

Lee, Laura, and Martyn Lee. *Absent Friend, Coping with the Loss of a Treasured Pet.* Bucks, England: Henston Ltd., 1992.

Montgomery, Herb, and Mary Montgomery. *Goodbye My Friend.* Minneapolis, MN: Montgomery Press, 1991.

Sife, Wallace. *The Loss of a Pet.* New York, NY: Howell Book House, John Wiley & Sons, 1998.

The American Veterinary Medical Association
Pet Loss Support Hotlines
www.avma.org/careforanimals/animatedjourneys/goodbyefriend

The Association for Pet Loss and Bereavement (APLB)
P.O. Box 106
Brooklyn, NY 11230
(718) 382-0690
aplb@aplb.org
www.aplb.org

Especially for children:

Rogers, Fred. *When a Pet Dies*. New York, NY: Penguin Putnam, 1998.

White, E. B. *Charlotte's Web*. New York, NY: HarperCollins Juvenile Books, 1999.

Viorst, Judith. *The Tenth Good Thing About Barney*. New York, NY: Aladdin Library, Simon & Shuster, 1976.

See also: WHAT IS GRIEF? UNDERSTANDING THE PROCESS OF MOURNING AND HOW YOU CAN HELP, WHAT CAN I SAY? COMMUNICATIONS THAT COMFORT, and WHAT CAN I DO? HOW TO LISTEN.

ELEVEN

Mental Illness

"He gives little who gives with a frown; he gives much
who gives little with a smile."

—Talmud

MENTAL illness shows no partiality to age, ethnicity, race, or financial standing. Mental illness, according to the National Mental Health Association, causes mild to severe disturbances in thought and/or behavior, resulting in an inability to cope with life's ordinary demands and routines. An estimated 54 million Americans suffer from some form of mental disorder in a given year.

Major depression, bipolar disorder, schizophrenia, and obsessive-compulsive disorder account for four of the ten leading causes of disability in the United States. Depression is the leading cause of disability; the National Institute of Mental Health reports that approximately 18.8 million American adults or about 9.5 percent of the population age eighteen and older have a depressive disorder in a given year. Nearly twice as many women (12.0 percent) as men (6.6 percent) in the United States are affected; these figures translate to 12.4 million women and 6.4 million men.

Mental illness is a contributing factor in suicide, a leading cause of death in the United States.

Individuals experiencing mental illness and their loved ones need your caring support. You can help them best by demonstrating your love and acceptance through verbal and nonverbal communications.

THINGS TO CONSIDER

- Mental illness can be difficult to diagnose and treat. It is essential to find a psychiatrist who will work well with both the individual and family members.

- Mental illness carries a stigma, but with proper care and treatment, many individuals can cope and recover.

- Medication, support systems, mental health programs, and vocational rehabilitation help many people lead productive lives.

- It is important to support parents, spouses, children, caregivers, and other family members of people with a mental disorder. These folks are often forgotten but bear burdens as well.

EMOTIONS AND FEELINGS TO ANTICIPATE

- Anger
- Denial
- Despair
- Exhaustion
- Fear
- Guilt
- Helplessness
- Inferiority
- Loneliness
- Misery
- Pain
- Panic
- Sadness
- Shame

WHAT TO SAY AND DO

- If a loved one is diagnosed with a mental illness, learn all you can about the particular mental illness, forms of treatment, and side effects.

- Access information and resources through your local mental health association. You can find these listed in the Yellow Pages of your local phone directory. Additional resources are also listed at the end of this chapter.

- Conduct research using the Internet. Access the websites listed at the end of this chapter.

- Speak with mental health professionals about the illness prognosis, coping techniques, and how you can help your loved one.

- Encourage your loved one to see a therapist or counselor.

- If they don't like the therapist or counselor, help them find one who is more compatible.

- Find support through your clergy, family physician, or family service agencies. Your clergy can help you identify resources in your area.

- Find supportive family members and friends to vent and share your feelings and frustrations.

- Research and locate support groups to find others who have coped with the same experiences and problems.

- Listen to your loved one.

- Set limits on how much time you will listen and what you can do to help them.

> ↝ If they accept an invitation and call at the last moment to cancel, communicate your disappointment. Let them know that if they need to cancel an invitation in the future, you would like more notice.

- Recognize your own limitations in what you can do.

- Hold them accountable for basic human courtesies.

- Retain your own interests, hobbies, relationships, and work experiences to keep your balance and perspective.

- Seek ways to minimize your stress through exercise, creative outlets, and supportive relationships.

- Know when and how to get help for yourself when you are overwhelmed with what your loved one is experiencing.

HOW TO SAY IT

I care about you.

I know I can never completely understand what you are going through, but I would like to try.

I love you.

I will be available Sunday afternoon.

I will be here for you.

It's never too late.

This must be painful for you.

You can count on me.

WHAT NOT TO SAY AND DO

- Do not offer to solve their problems.

- Do not tell them what to do.

- Don't criticize.

- Don't shut them out.

- Don't deprive them of your love and support.

- Don't ignore them.

- Don't take on more than you can handle.

HOW NOT TO SAY IT

Count your blessings.

If you think you have problems . . .

Don't worry.

What will we tell people?

Just forget about it.

You're being silly.

For further information:

Adamec, Christine. *How to Live with a Mentally Ill Person*. New York, NY: John Wiley & Sons, 1996.

Bockian, Neil R., Nora Elizabeth Villagran, and Valerie Porr. *New Hope for People with Borderline Personality Disorder: Your Friendly, Authoritative Guide to the Latest in Traditional and Complementary Solutions.* Roseville, CA: Prima Publishing, 2002.

Carter, Rosalynn, with Susan K. Golant. *Helping Someone with Mental Illness.* New York, NY: Times Books, 1999.

Golant, Mitch, and Susan K. Golant. *What to Do When Someone You Love Is Depressed.* New York, NY: Henry Holt & Company, Inc., 1998.

Karp, David Allen. *The Burden of Sympathy: How Families Cope with Mental Illness.* Oxford, England: Oxford University Press, 2001.

Mason, Paul T., M.S., and Randi Kreger. *Stop Walking on Eggshells—Taking Your Life Back When Someone You Care About Has Borderline Personality Disorder.* Oakland, CA: New Harbinger Publications, 1998.

Miklowitz, David J. *The Bipolar Disorder Survival Guide: What You and Your Family Need to Know.* New York, NY: Guildford Press, 2002.

Nasar, Sylvia. *A Beautiful Mind: The Life of Mathematical Genius and Nobel Laureate John Nash.* New York, NY: Simon & Schuster, 2001.

O'Connor, Richard. *Undoing Depression: What Therapy Doesn't Teach You and Medication Can't Give You.* New York, NY: Berkley Publishing Group, 1999.

Olen, Dale R., Ph.D. *Defeating Depression—Lifting Yourself from Sadness to Joy.* Holmes Beach, FL: Learning Publications, 2003.

National Alliance for the Mentally Ill (NAMI)
Colonial Place Three
2107 Wilson Boulevard, Suite 300
Arlington, VA 22201
(703) 524-7600
NAMI HelpLine: 1 (800) 950-NAMI
www.nami.org

National Institute of Mental Health (NIMH)
6001 Executive Boulevard, Room 8184, MSC 9663
Bethesda, MD 20892-9663

(301) 443-4513 or toll-free (866) 615-NIMH
www.nimh.nih.gov

National Mental Health Association
2001 N. Beauregard Street, 12th Floor
Alexandria, VA 22311
(703) 684-7722
www.nmha.org

See also: WHAT CAN I SAY? COMMUNICATIONS THAT COMFORT and WHAT CAN I DO? HOW TO LISTEN.

COMMUNICATING IN THE FACE OF CRIME AND VIOLENCE

Nothing in life prepares us for the shocking experience of crime and violence—the feelings of sorrow, helplessness, and loss are devastating, and the aftermath of crime and violence may last for years. Support is crucial to the healing process, but grief can be intense and prolonged, taxing even the most loyal supporters.

You can help your loved one, friend, co-worker, or community member cope with crime and violence by remaining patient and understanding. Your consistent presence, for however long it takes, can help them through this traumatic experience.

Part Four provides specific insight into nonviolent crime, violent crime, sexual assault or rape, domestic violence, natural disasters, terrorism, and legal or criminal problems, with guidelines on verbal, written, and nonverbal communications that are sure to comfort.

TWELVE

Nonviolent Crime

"It is one of the most beautiful compensations
of life, that no man can sincerely try to help another
without helping himself."

—Ralph Waldo Emerson

ACROSS the United States, nonviolent crimes have declined since 1973. Although these statistics are heartening, if you happen to be a victim of property or nonviolent crime, the experience can be devastating. Other property and nonviolent crime statistics by the Bureau of Justice Statistics indicate:

- Property crime, consisting of burglary, theft, and motor vehicle theft, makes up about three-quarters of all crime in the United States.

- In 2001, 78 percent of males and 51 percent of females reported the individual who robbed them was a stranger.

- About 85 percent of burglaries were successful.

- About 72 percent of all motor vehicle thefts were successful.

- Of the 13.7 million completed thefts of property in 2001, there were 4.7 million property thefts of less than $50, 4.8 million thefts between $50 and $249, and 3.2 million thefts of $250 or more.

Victims of nonviolent crime are fortunate they were not physically hurt, but their psyche is badly shaken. They will need your help and support to regain a sense of control and security.

VICTIM OR SURVIVOR?

You will find differing opinions on the appropriate way to identify the person upon whom a crime was perpetrated. Some people feel they should be called a "survivor," which is more empowering. Others prefer to be identified as "victims of crime." For the purpose of unity, this chapter and Chapter Thirteen (Violent Crime) will refer to crime victims as "victims of crime."

THINGS TO CONSIDER

- The type of crime.

- The victim's personal and financial needs as a result of the crime.

- Victims of any type of crime feel personally violated.

- The damage to the victim's psyche even though no one was physically injured.

- Reactions to traumatic events can last a long time.

- There is no single standard of coping; each person is unique and copes in their own way and in their own time.

EMOTIONS AND FEELINGS TO ANTICIPATE

- Anxiety
- Deep anger
- Disorientation
- Fear
- Guilt
- Insecurity
- Pain
- Powerlessness
- Shock
- Terror
- Violation
- Vulnerability

WHAT TO SAY AND DO

- Communicate that you really do want to listen, and try to really hear what the victim of crime is saying.

- Do try and get a sense from the conversation as to what the victim of crime needs from you; it might just be someone to listen.

- Ask if they would like to stay with you or have you stay with them until they are feeling safer.

- Do let them know that whatever they are feeling is a normal response to their experience.

- Do understand their fear and how shaken they are.

> ॐ Offer to research resources for victims of crime or, if you have knowledge of resources for victims of crime, provide them to the victim.

- Validate that it is okay to get help if they are unable to cope with their feelings and fears.

HOW TO SAY IT

How are you feeling?

How can I help you?

I am really sorry this has happened.

I am sorry you have been through something so frightening.

I'd like to help in any way I can.

This must be very hard for you.

Whatever you did was the right thing.

You are not at fault.

You couldn't have known.

WHAT NOT TO SAY AND DO

- Don't assume that there was something they could have done differently to prevent the crime.

- Don't ask questions that cause the victim to blame themselves for what happened.

- Don't second-guess the decision the victim made that might have made them or their property vulnerable.

- Don't try to find something good in the crime experience, such as "You are lucky you weren't in the car when it happened."

- Don't try to minimize the crime experience, such as "It could have been so much worse."

- Don't make them feel that they were at fault for the crime by telling them what they could have done differently and what they should do in the future to avoid this type of situation.

HOW NOT TO SAY IT

At least you weren't hurt.

Didn't you bolt the door?

How could it have happened?

I told you that wasn't a good neighborhood.

I've told you before not to talk to strangers.

Look on the bright side . . .

Why didn't you lock your car?

You could have been really hurt.

SAMPLE LETTERS/E-MAILS

To a friend whose home was burglarized.

> January X, 2XXX
> Dear Toni:
>
> I was saddened to hear your home was burglarized. What a frightening experience to go through. I am thankful that you were all out of the house at the time and none of you were harmed.
>
> It is awful to go through this type of experience and have your safety and personal space violated. Allow yourself to experience and work through your feelings and emotions. Give yourself time to heal, and do whatever you need to do to feel safe again.

I will be in your area during spring break. I would love to see you then, but in the meantime, know that you are in my thoughts. Take good care of yourself.

Love,
Sheila

To a daughter whose car was stolen.

October X, 2XXX
Dear Stella:

I hope things have settled down since we last spoke. Dad told me you rented a car and took care of all the required notifications.

This was an awful experience for you, Stella, and I am so sorry you had to go through it. Losing your beloved Volvo along with your personal papers is a terrible loss. As sad as it is, I am so very grateful that you were not injured. You can replace the material things, Stella, but you yourself are irreplaceable.

Know that Dad and I are thinking of you. Please plan on having dinner with us on Thursday. I will fix the spaghetti dinner you love so much. Until then I send my love.

Mom

For further information:

Levy, Naomi. *To Begin Again—The Journey Toward Comfort, Strength, and Faith in Difficult Times.* New York, NY: Ballantine Books, 1998.

Matsakis, Aphrodite, Ph.D. *I Can't Get Over It: A Handbook for Trauma Survivors, Second Edition.* Oakland, CA: New Harbinger Publications Inc., 1996.

National Center for Victims of Crime
2000 M Street, NW, Suite 480
Washington, DC 20036
(202) 467-8700
www.ncvc.org

National Organization for Victim Assistance (NOVA)
1730 Park Road NW
Washington, DC 20010

(202) 232-6682

Information and referrals for victims of crime and disaster (800) TRY-NOVA

www.try-nova.org

Victim Services Helpline
(800) FYI-CALL
gethelp@ncvc.org

See also: WHAT IS GRIEF? UNDERSTANDING THE PROCESS OF MOURNING AND HOW YOU CAN HELP, WHAT CAN I SAY? COMMUNICATIONS THAT COMFORT, and WHAT CAN I DO? HOW TO LISTEN.

THIRTEEN

Violent Crime

*"A real friend is one who walks in when the
rest of the world walks out."*

—Walter Winchell

NOTHING in life prepares us for the traumatic experience of violent crime such as homicide, rape, sexual assault, or domestic violence. Although violent crime rates have declined in recent years, the Federal Bureau of Investigation reports that in the United States in 2000, one violent crime occurred every 22.1 seconds, one aggravated assault occurred every 34.6 seconds, and someone was murdered every 33.9 minutes.

Victims of violence and their families and friends experience crisis reactions; the levels of extremes will differ from person to person based on their personal situation at the time of the crime, the impact of the crime, and resulting injuries. As each person is unique, so are victim reactions, responses, and recovery. It is impossible to compare one experience, response, or recovery to another.

How the victim of crime and their loved ones are treated immediately following the crime impacts their ability to cope and recover. They will need to know what comes next by way of the crime investigation and the resulting criminal justice process.

In times of crisis, friends, acquaintances, and loved ones willingly provide support. But support wanes along with the months, and it is easy to lose patience as time passes. You can play a pivotal role in the recovery process by remaining a presence in their life—no matter how long it takes.

The topics of sexual assault and rape are covered in Chapter Fourteen.

The topic of domestic violence is covered in Chapter Fifteen.

VICTIM OR SURVIVOR?

You will find differing opinions on the appropriate way to identify the person upon whom a crime was perpetrated. Some people feel they should be called a "survivor," which is more empowering. Others prefer to be identified as "victims of crime." For the purpose of unity, this chapter and Chapter Twelve (Nonviolent Crime) will refer to crime victims as "victims of crime."

THINGS TO CONSIDER

- Victims of crime will experience both physical and psychological trauma.

- It is imperative that victims of crime regain a sense of safety and develop outlets to express their emotions.

- Victims of crime might have financial difficulties resulting from the crime—there might be uncovered medical expenses, counseling services, property loss, funeral expenses, transportation costs, and unpaid employment leave to participate in the criminal justice system and attend court. There might also be a significant income loss.

- Victims of crime must be treated with dignity, compassion, and respect to facilitate recovery.

- There is no single standard of coping; each person is unique and copes in their own way and in their own time.

EMOTIONS AND FEELINGS TO ANTICIPATE

- Anger
- Anxiety
- Denial
- Devastation
- Distrust
- Fear
- Guilt
- Helplessness
- Hopelessness
- Humiliation
- Hurt
- Injustice
- Insecurity
- Irritability
- Isolation
- Loss
- Numbness
- Rage

- Sadness
- Self-blame
- Shame

- Shock
- Terror
- Vulnerability

WHAT TO SAY AND DO

- Express sympathy and sorrow for what has happened.

- Anyone who has lost a loved one to a violent crime will need your caring patience. It takes a long time to heal, and they will need your support during the process.

- Anger is a natural response to a violent crime. Listen with patience; the victim of crime is not looking for answers but an opportunity to vent their anger.

> ↬ Offer to help with the basic necessities—grocery shopping, cleaning, laundry, food preparation, child care, and carpooling—as they might find it impossible to resume their normal housekeeping and caregiver tasks.

- Recognize that they will grieve in their own way.

- Do communicate your willingness to support the victim of crime in whatever ways you can. Individuals who have someone to lean on increase their chances of healing from the trauma.

- Locate victim assistance services through your local police department.

- Offer to help research other community and counseling support services.

- Encourage them to participate in the judicial process to restore a sense of control.

- Offer to listen. The individual will need to tell their story over and over again to process what has happened.

- Allow them to grieve in their own way.

- Encourage them to express their grief and sorrow for as long as they need.

- Those who experience violent crime are changed; many victims of crime find that they reconstruct and change their lives in the aftermath and recovery process. Support them and accept the changes.

- Do continue to keep in touch with them and remember them during significant dates and difficult periods, such as the anniversary of the crime, a birthday, or holidays.

HOW TO SAY IT

I am here for you when you need me.

I care about you and will support you however you might need me.

I have never experienced this before; please let me know how I can help you.

I will always be your friend; nothing can change that.

I will miss him (her), too.

I'd like to help any way I can.

I'm glad you survived.

It's not your fault.

This was a terrible crime, and I am sorry it happened to you.

What you are feeling is normal.

You are safe now.

You can talk to me at any time.

You did the best you could.

You were in no way to blame for what happened.

WHAT NOT TO SAY AND DO

- Don't disbelieve their account of the crime.

- Don't be alarmed with their anger or rage. It is a natural expression, and they must voice their anger and life's unfairness if they are to heal.

- Stay clear of questions that begin with the word *why*—these questions tend to put the blame on the victim rather than the assailant.

- Don't judge the victim of crime in what has happened, their response, or how they are handling their grief.

- Don't try to hurry their grief along. They need the time to heal in their own way and at their own speed.

- Avoid telling the victim of crime how you would have reacted in the same situation.

- Don't ask for details. The event might be too painful for them to share.

- Don't suggest they could have avoided the crime by doing something different.

HOW NOT TO SAY IT

How could you have let them into your house?

How could you have trusted him (her)?

It's time to move on.

What was he doing there?

Why did you go there?

Why didn't you fight back?

Why were you there in the first place?

You need to get over it.

SAMPLE LETTER/E-MAIL

To a friend who was badly injured in an assault.

September X, 2XXX
Dear Will:

You have constantly been in my thoughts and prayers these last few days, and I have been struggling to find some words to comfort you. I am at a loss at how this could have happened and how I can best help you.

There have been so many times when you sat and listened to me and lent me your shoulder to cry on. You didn't offer advice or comment on my woes; you just let me talk endlessly until I either exhausted myself or somehow figured out a solution. Your very presence was the solace I needed, and that is what I would like to give to you.

Mary told me you weren't up to having visitors, and it might be a while before you will see anyone. I have patience, and when you are ready to see me, I will be available. I will help you in any way you wish, and I'm in this with you for the long haul.

In the meantime, I will continue to pray for your recovery and keep in touch by mail. I send love and comfort to you, Will. Get well soon.

Love,
Meredith

For further information:

Doka, Kenneth J., Ph.D., ed. *Living with Grief After Sudden Loss: Suicide, Homicide, Accident, Heart Attack, Stroke.* Bristol, PA: Taylor & Francis, 1996.

Levy, Naomi. *To Begin Again—The Journey Toward Comfort, Strength, and Faith in Difficult Times.* New York, NY: Ballantine Books, 1998.

Matsakis, Aphrodite, Ph.D. *I Can't Get Over It: A Handbook for Trauma Survivors, Second Edition.* Oakland, CA: New Harbinger Publications, Inc., 1996.

Wolfelt, Alan D., Ph.D. *Healing Your Traumatized Heart: 100 Practical Ideas After Someone You Love Dies a Sudden, Violent Death.* Fort Collins, CO: Companion Press, 2002.

Department of Justice, Office for Victims of Crime (OVC)
www.ojp.usdoj.gov/ovc

Families and Friends of Violent Crime Victims
P.O. Box 1949
Everett, WA 98206
(425) 355-6822
(800) 346-7555
www.fnfvcv.org

Mothers Against Drunk Driving (MADD)
669 Airport Freeway, Suite 310

Hurst, TX 76053
(817) 268-MADD

National Center for Victims of Crime
2000 M Street, NW, Suite 480
Washington, DC 20036
(202) 467-8700
www.ncvc.org

The National Coalition of Homicide Survivors, Inc.
www.mivictims.org/nchs

National Organization for Victim Assistance (NOVA)
1730 Park Road NW
Washington, DC 20010
(202) 232-6682
Information and referrals for victims of crime and disaster (800) TRY-NOVA
www.try-nova.org

National Organization of Parents of Murdered Children (POMC)
100 East Eighth Street, Suite B-41
Cincinnati, OH 45202
(513) 721-LOVE or (513) 242-8025

The Compassionate Friends, Inc.
National Headquarters
P.O. Box 3696
Oak Brook, IL 60522-3696
(630) 990-0010 or (877) 969-0010
www.compassionatefriends.org

Victim Services Helpline
(800) FYI-CALL
gethelp@ncvc.org

See also: WHAT IS GRIEF? UNDERSTANDING THE PROCESS OF MOURNING AND HOW YOU CAN HELP, WHAT CAN I SAY? COMMUNICATIONS THAT COMFORT, WHAT CAN I DO? HOW TO LISTEN, NONVIOLENT CRIME, SEXUAL ASSAULT OR RAPE, and DOMESTIC VIOLENCE.

FOURTEEN

Sexual Assault or Rape

"You can't live a perfect day without doing something for someone who will never be able to repay you."

—John Wooden

ACCORDING to the American Medical Association, sexual assault or rape is one of the most rapidly growing and most serious violent crimes in the United States. The Federal Bureau of Investigation reports that in the United States in 2000, a forcible rape occurred every 5.8 minutes. Often unreported, rape is referred to as a silent crime.

Sexual assault or rape can be committed by an unknown offender, an acquaintance or someone known to the victim, or by a marital partner. According to a 2001 report issued by the U.S. Department of Justice, Bureau of Justice Statistics, six in ten sexual assault or rape survivors stated they knew the offender as an intimate, other relative, friend, or acquaintance.

When a sexual assault or rape is committed by someone known to the survivor, it is referred to as acquaintance rape. When sexual assault or rape occurs on a date or between two individuals who expect to or who already have an intimate relationship, it is referred to as date rape.

Females aged sixteen to twenty-four appear most vulnerable according to a U.S. Department of Justice, Bureau of Justice Statistics report. They experienced the highest per capita rates of intimate violence—19.6 victimizations per 1,000 females.

The sexual assault and rape numbers are staggering. A study conducted in 1992 by the National Center for Victims of Crime and Crime Victims Research and Treatment Center states that 12.1 million American women have been victims of forcible rape.

Women are not the only victims of sexual assault and rape; these same crimes are committed against males. The American Academy of Pediatrics estimates that 5 percent of committed sexual assaults are against men.

Although they might be fortunate to have survived rape or sexual assault, those who survive violent crimes aren't feeling lucky. They'll need your continuous support, so check in with them frequently to see how they are doing and let them know you are there for them.

VICTIM OR SURVIVOR?

There is a real dispute among professionals whether victims of crime are victims per se or survivors. I took all the comments and decided victims of crime was appropriate for Chapters Twelve and Thirteen, but for rape, survivor was more empowering. I felt "survivor" was certainly not an appropriate term for domestic violence—the "abused" or "victim of domestic violence" seemed most appropriate. The four chapters are very different and I wanted to show their distinction rather than treating them all under one umbrella.

THINGS TO CONSIDER

- Studies estimate that as many as one in eight women may be sexually assaulted in their lifetime.

- Sexual assault or rape survivors might feel so embarrassed or shamed by the experience that they tell no one and withdraw socially.

- Many rapes go unreported or survivors are unwilling to press charges because they know the assailant and are afraid they will be harassed by them and/or mutual friends.

- Sexual crimes against men are frequently underreported; men are less willing to press charges and have a greater fear of the criminal justice system and how their case will be handled.

EMOTIONS AND FEELINGS TO ANTICIPATE

- Anger
- Confusion
- Denial
- Depression

- Disbelief
- Embarrassment
- Fear
- Frustration
- Guilt
- Helplessness
- Hopelessness
- Humiliation
- Insecurity

- Irritability
- Numbness
- Panic
- Self-blame
- Shame
- Shock
- Terror
- Violation
- Worry

WHAT TO SAY AND DO

- Recommend that they contact a sexual assault crisis center. The Rape, Abuse, and Incest National Network (RAINN) 24-hour hotline at (800) 656-HOPE will help you find a center near you.

- Suggest that they report the assault, but don't push it. If the survivor resists, let it go.

- Encourage them to seek medical care.

- Offer to accompany them to the police station or the hospital.

- Help them find any information they might need by way of phone numbers or support and counseling services.

- If the survivor has children, offer to watch the children while they report the assault.

- Let them make their own choices; this will help them regain control of their life.

- Let them know that they do not have to face this alone.

- Consistently be there for them.

- Let them know that whenever they would like to talk, you will be ready to listen.

- Be willing to listen without judging.

- Communicate that you believe them.

- Allow them to speak at their own pace; don't try to hurry them along.

- Reinforce that it is not their fault the assault occurred; no one asks to be sexually assaulted or raped.

- Ask them what you can do to make them feel comfortable.

- Ask if there is anyone you can call for them.

- Offer to stay with them or take them to your home.

- Validate their feelings; let them know that whatever they are feeling is okay.

- Encourage them to seek professional help if they are unable to talk about the assault.

> ∼ If you have difficulty dealing with the sexual assault or the emotional response, you can also call the local sexual assault center to learn how you can handle your own feelings and the survivor's emotions while providing the needed support.

HOW TO SAY IT

I love you and care about you.

I will help you in any way you need me to.

I'd like to help if I can.

If you ever want to talk about it, I am here for you.

It wasn't your fault.

Please let me know how I can help you.

This doesn't change the wonderful person you are.

We'll get through this together.

Whatever you are feeling is okay.

Whatever you did was the right thing for you at the time.

When you are ready to talk, I am here.

You are not to blame.

You can talk to me any time.

You couldn't have known.

You didn't ask for it.

WHAT NOT TO SAY AND DO

- Don't suggest they were to blame for the assault. Under no circumstances were they at fault.

- Don't imply that they could have done something different, such as kicking the assailant or running, that would have prevented the attack.

- If you are uncomfortable with what has happened, don't demonstrate your discomfort by way of your body language and your approach to the survivor.

- Don't imply that it wasn't rape because they knew the assailant.

- Don't avoid the survivor once they have told you what has happened. If you choose to stay away, they might interpret your actions incorrectly. Your absence might signal that you don't believe them or that you are shocked or repelled by their experience.

- Don't finish their sentences. They might speak slowly, and it is important to allow them time to control their emotions and form their own thoughts.

- Don't criticize the survivor for the clothing they wore, their circle of friends or acquaintances, what they said, or where they were when the assault occurred.

- Don't imply that the survivor used poor judgment in their behavior, despite the circumstances they might have put themselves in prior to the assault. Even if they drank or had too much to drink, they did not provoke the assault or deserve to be assaulted. No one deserves to be raped.

- Avoid any statements beginning with "If you had only." This implies that the survivor rather than the assailant is to blame.

- Don't pressure them to talk. They do need to talk about the experience, but they will talk about it when they are ready.

- Don't push for details of the assault. It might be too painful to share or too embarrassing. If they want to share this information with you, they will do so when they are ready.

- Don't tell anyone what has happened without first obtaining permission. It is important to respect their right to privacy.

- Don't criticize how they handled themselves.

- Don't tell them how you would have handled it.

- Don't tell them it would have never happened to you.

- Don't judge them.

- Don't try to relate it to yourself. Your story is not their story. This is about them, not you.

- Don't look at the survivor any differently than you did before.

- Don't suggest that the survivor is damaged goods because of the assault.

- Don't ask them how it could have happened without their consent. Sexual assault or rape is a violent crime of power and control; it has nothing to do with sexual desire.

- Don't touch them without asking, even a hug. The survivor's personal space was violated, and because you don't know exactly what happened during the assault, you might inadvertently touch them in a way that triggers reminders of what happened.

- Don't behave differently when you are with them.

- Don't act as if you pity them. They need your loving care and concern, not your pity.

HOW NOT TO SAY IT

How could it have happened?

I feel sorry for you.

I told you he wasn't good for you.

I told you not to drink so much.

I wish you hadn't gone to that party.

If only you didn't dress so suggestively.

She was asking for it.

This was my greatest fear, and now it's happened.

What exactly happened?

Why didn't you yell?

SAMPLE LETTERS/E-MAILS

To a college friend who has experienced date rape.

> June X, 2XXX
> Dear Diane:
>
> You have been in my thoughts all morning. I am so sorry that such a terrible thing happened to someone as special as you. I know this is a difficult time, and although I do not fully understand what you are going through, please know that I want to be there for you in any way I can. If you want company, I will be there; if you want to talk, I want to listen.
>
> How about if we plan to be together this weekend? I could fix that chicken dish you like so much, and you can spend the night if you like.
>
> Know that I will be thinking of you today. I will call you later so you can let me know what I can do to help. Take care, stay strong, and I will see you soon.
>
> I love you,
> Jo Ann

To a friend who has been sexually assaulted.

February X, 2XXX
Dear Anna:

I left you a message today, but I wanted to write as well to let you know that I have been thinking about you. I know this is an extremely difficult time for you, but I also know that you are strong and will get through this. Please remember, though, that you don't have to get through it alone. You are surrounded by family and friends who love you and want to support you in any way we can.

No one knows better than you how much it hurts, so I won't pretend to know how you feel. But I do know that the pain you are feeling is part of the grieving process. Allow yourself to work through your feelings at your own pace. It might not seem like it now, but you will feel better with time.

I understand that the Sexual Assault Center's support group has helped many rape survivors cope with feelings of loss and distrust. If you'd like, I can go with you to a meeting. If you aren't ready now, we can talk about it later.

Anna, you are a beautiful, intelligent, and loving woman. No one can take that away from you. I am here for you. Call me anytime, day or night, if you want company or just want to talk.

I love you,
Lynne

For further information:

Aranow, Vicki, C.S.W., and Monique Lang, C.S.W. *Journey to Wholeness—Healing from the Trauma of Rape.* Holmes Beach, FL: Learning Publications, 2000.

Ledray, Linda E. *Recovering from Rape.* New York, NY: Henry Holt & Company, 1986.

Levy, Naomi. *To Begin Again—The Journey Toward Comfort, Strength, and Faith in Difficult Times.* New York, NY: Ballantine Books, 1998.

Sebold, Alice. *Lucky: A Memoir.* New York, NY: Scribner, 1999.

Warshaw, Robin. *I Never Called It Rape: The Ms. Report on Recognizing, Fighting, and Surviving Date and Acquaintance Rape.* New York, NY: HarperCollins Publishers, 1994.

Department of Justice, Office for Victims of Crime (OVC)
www.ojp.usdoj.gov/ovc

National Center for Victims of Crime
2000 M Street, NW, Suite 480
Washington, DC 20036
(202) 467-8700
www.ncvc.org

National Organization for Victim Assistance (NOVA)
1730 Park Road NW
Washington, DC 20010
(202) 232-6682
Information and referrals for victims of crime and disaster (800) TRY-NOVA
www.try-nova.org

The Rape, Abuse, and Incest National Network (RAINN) 24-hour hotline
(800) 656-HOPE
www.rainn.org

Victim Services Helpline
(800) FYI-CALL
gethelp@ncvc.org

See also: WHAT IS GRIEF? UNDERSTANDING THE PROCESS OF MOURNING AND HOW YOU CAN HELP, WHAT CAN I SAY? COMMUNICATIONS THAT COMFORT, WHAT CAN I DO? HOW TO LISTEN, and VIOLENT CRIME.

FIFTEEN

Domestic Violence

"Good friends are good for your health."

—Irwin Sarason

IN a report issued by the U.S. Department of Justice, Bureau of Justice Statistics, domestic violence is defined as violent crimes by current or former spouses, boyfriends, or girlfriends. Violent crimes include lethal (homicide) and nonlethal (rape, sexual assault, robbery, aggravated assault, and simple assault) offenses.

Studies by the Surgeon General's office and reported in the *Journal of the American Medical Association* reveal that domestic violence is the leading cause of injury to women between the ages of fifteen and forty-four; domestic violence is a more common cause of death to this age group than automobile accidents, muggings, and cancer combined.

In a survey conducted by the Commonwealth Fund in 1998, almost one third of American women reported being sexually or physically abused by a spouse or boyfriend at some point in their lives.

Another report issued by the U.S. Department of Justice, Bureau of Justice Statistics provides startling facts about domestic violence:

- Women were much more likely to be victims of domestic violence, experiencing more than ten times as many incidents of violence by an intimate than males.

- Six times as many women victimized by intimates (18 percent) as those victimized by strangers (3 percent) did not report their violent victimization to police because they feared offender reprisal.

- Nearly two in three female victims of violence were related to or knew their attacker.

If you suspect that someone you care about might be a victim of domestic violence, she (or he) might not be ready to take control of their situation. The abused have every reason to fear retribution if they report the crime, and they are likely to be financially dependent on the abuser.

Although it might be frustrating to see someone you care about struggling in this type of situation, remain actively understanding and empathetic. They desperately need your steadfast support if they are to break this violent cycle.

VICTIM OR SURVIVOR?

You will find differing opinions on the appropriate way to identify the person upon whom a crime was perpetrated. Some people feel they should be called a "survivor," which is more empowering. Others prefer to be identified as "victims of crime." This chapter will refer to crime victims as "victims of domestic violence" or as "the abused."

THINGS TO CONSIDER

- Domestic abuse is a silent crime; a great many cases go unreported.

- Domestic abuse isn't just committed against women; about 5 percent of reported cases are committed by women against men.

- Physical abuse, such as a punch, slap, or shove, isn't the only form of abuse. Domestic violence can take the form of verbal or emotional abuse by way of threats, intimidation, domination, or isolation. It can also take the form of financial abuse by way of controlling or concealing money or joint assets.

- Domination or control in the areas of religion, spirituality, sex, or social relationships also constitutes domestic abuse.

- Stalking is a form of abusive behavior, and the majority of cases involve women being stalked by ex-husbands or former boyfriends.

EMOTIONS AND FEELINGS TO ANTICIPATE

- Denial
- Dependency
- Embarrassment
- Fear for safety
- Fear of retribution
- Guilt
- Helplessness

- Humiliation
- Incompetency
- Insecurity
- Isolation
- Self-blame
- Shame
- Terror

WHAT TO SAY AND DO

- Demonstrate your concern if someone you care about is in an abusive situation, but be careful—domestic violence is a deadly crime.

- Encourage them to deal with a professional who can help them assess their personal situation.

- If the abused is having difficulty accessing information, call the National Domestic Violence Hotline yourself to secure the latest information to pass on.

> ↪ Recommend they locate and contact professionals at domestic violence hotlines. The National Domestic Violence Hotline is 1(800) 799-SAFE and is available twenty-four hours a day.

- Communicate your willingness and availability to listen.

- Offer support, and be empathetic and understanding.

- If you are told about abuse, reinforce that you believe the abused.

- Research and identify available community services through your local phone book.

- Call the Department of Social Services to learn about domestic violence services such as crisis counseling, medical care, legal assistance or advocacy, shelters, housing, or employment.

- Contact these organizations and find out what they provide for someone experiencing domestic abuse. Record key information in a notebook.

- Locate support groups.

- Suggest the abused change their routines.

- Recommend that they prepare a safety plan before they experience a crisis; an effective plan establishes ways to reduce risk.

HOW TO SAY IT

How can I help you?

I am concerned about you.

I am concerned about your safety.

I care about you.

I have no experience with this, so you will have to let me know what I can do to help you.

I would like to help you.

If you would like to talk, I'm available to listen.

Is there something I can do to help?

No one deserves to be hurt by someone else.

You are a wonderful person.

You are not to blame.

You did not cause this.

WHAT NOT TO SAY AND DO

- Don't blame the abused.

- Don't say anything that makes the abused think you don't believe them.

- Don't question their ability to make it on their own.

- Don't act judgmental if someone shares a domestic violence experience with you that happened long ago.

- Don't make someone feel guilty for not taking action against prior abuse.

- Don't give conditional support, for example "I will only help you if you leave him."

HOW NOT TO SAY IT

Get out while you can.

Have you no shame?

How can you stand this?

I can't believe he (she) would do this.

What are you doing to anger them?

Where is your pride?

Special Situations

My co-worker comes to work every Monday with bruises.
Approach your supervisor and tell them that your co-worker shows up with bruises every Monday morning. The organization you work for should have procedures in place to handle this type of problem. Let your supervisor be the one to take charge of the situation.

For further information:

Brown, Louis, Francois Dubau, and Merritt McKeon, J.D. *Stop Domestic Violence: An Action Plan for Saving Lives.* New York, NY: St. Martin's Press, 1997.

Cook, Philip W. *Abused Men: The Hidden Side of Domestic Violence.* Portsmouth, NH: Praeger Trade, 1997.

Dugan, Meg Kennedy, A.M., and Roger R. Hock, Ph.D. *It's My Life Now—Starting Over After an Abusive Relationship or Domestic Violence.* New York, NY: Routledge, 2000.

Lissette, Andrea, M.A. C.D.V.C., and Richard Kraus, Ph.D. *Free Yourself from an Abusive Relationship.* Alameda, CA: Hunter House Publishers, 1999.

Nicarthy, Ginny, M.S.W. *Getting Free: You Can End Abuse and Take Back Your Life.* Seattle, WA: Seal Press, 1997.

Rosenberg, Marshall B., Ph.D. *Nonviolent Communication: A Language of Life, Second Edition.* Encinitas, CA: PuddleDancer Press, 2003.

Statman, Jan Berliner. *The Battered Woman's Survival Guide.* Dallas, TX: Taylor Publishing Company, 1995.

Center for Nonviolent Communication
www.cnvc.org/main.htm

Department of Justice, Office for Victims of Crime (OVC)
www.ojp.usdoj.gov/ovc

National Organization for Victim Assistance (NOVA)
1730 Park Road NW
Washington, DC 20010
(202) 232-6682
Information and referrals for victims of crime and disaster (800) TRY-NOVA
www.try-nova.org

The National Coalition Against Domestic Violence
www.ncadv.org

The National Domestic Violence Hotline
(800) 799-SAFE, available twenty-four hours a day

See also: WHAT IS GRIEF? UNDERSTANDING THE PROCESS OF MOURNING AND HOW YOU CAN HELP, WHAT CAN I SAY? COMMUNICATIONS THAT COMFORT, WHAT CAN I DO? HOW TO LISTEN, and VIOLENT CRIME.

SIXTEEN

Natural Disasters

*"Kindness is gladdening the hearts of those who are
traveling in the dark with us."*

—Henri-Frederic Amiel

Each year, millions of people find themselves in the wrong place at the wrong time, encountering a wide range of natural disasters such as floods, hurricanes, tornadoes, earthquakes, mud slides, wildfires, volcanic eruptions, and blizzards.

Those who make it through these disasters might have experienced the death of loved ones, personal injuries, and/or potential loss of their home, employment, earthly possessions, and communities. They might have witnessed extremes in physical harm, injuries, or death. The more extensive the loss and trauma, the greater the risk for severe stress symptoms and lasting readjustment problems.

Although they might be fortunate to have survived, they will need a great deal of help and support in restoring their lives.

THINGS TO CONSIDER

- Despite warnings, natural disasters are always unexpected.

- No matter how prepared one is for the natural disaster, the actual event puts survivors at risk for psychological and readjustment problems.

- The National Center for Post Traumatic Stress Disorder (PTSD) reports that as many as one in three disaster survivors experience some or all of the following severe stress symptoms, which may lead to lasting PTSD, anxiety disorders, or depression: blank periods of time with no memory, nightmares, flashbacks, extreme attempts to avoid disturbing memories, extreme emotional numbing, panic attacks, rage, severe anxiety, and/or severe depression.

EMOTIONS AND FEELINGS TO ANTICIPATE

- Anxiety
- Confusion
- Desperation
- Disorientation
- Dislocation
- Grief
- Helplessness

- Fear
- Numbness
- Resentment
- Self-blame
- Shock
- Sorrow

WHAT TO SAY AND DO

- Offer safe shelter.

- Ensure that the survivor has privacy to reflect quietly and get some sleep.

- Locate and contact the local and state health departments to identify services for survivors.

> ꙮ Help the survivor contact disaster-relief agencies to secure help in restoring their lives. The resources listed at the end of this chapter provide support in cleanup, health, housing, and basic emergency assistance.

- Provide whatever help is needed as soon as it is safe, such as retrieving belongings after a tornado or flood; don't wait to be asked.

- Assess the survivor's condition, and provide support if they are injured. For suggestions on what you can do to help, see Chapter Four.

- Help connect them with other survivors to share their experiences and learn coping mechanisms.

- Be patient with the survivor, encouraging them to share their feelings and experience when they are ready.

- Be a willing listener. Allow the survivor to tell their story as often as they would like. Repeating their story over and over will help the survivor in the healing process.

- Let the survivor set the pace and speak as slowly as they need to in gathering their thoughts.

- Help them transition back into healthy living habits.

- Encourage good nutrition and restoration of wholesome eating patterns.

- Assist them in securing comfortable clothing that they will enjoy wearing, as they might have left their home quickly or experienced damage to personal belongings.

- Help them find quiet and undisturbed places to sleep so they can resume normal sleeping patterns.

- Encourage the survivor to get as much exercise as possible. Exercise is a great tool in coping with stress. Offer to accompany them on a walk, a swim, or at formal exercise classes.

- Give them a gift certificate for a relaxing massage.

- Allow them to cry.

- If they enjoy reading, encourage them to read the types of books that relax them or suggest rereading an old favorite.

- Suggest the survivor see a physician.

- Survivors might need more help coping with the trauma. Help them find a counselor or therapist, and accompany them to appointments if they need extra support.

HOW TO SAY IT

Come and stay with me.

I am here to listen whenever you need to talk.

I am so grateful you are okay.

I will help you any way I can.

Of course you are shaken; I would be, too.

This must have been a terrible shock.

What can I do to help you?

You can count on us for whatever you need.

You couldn't have known.

You did the best you could in the circumstances.

WHAT NOT TO SAY AND DO

- Don't tell them they are "lucky" because they survived. If they have lost their home, prized possessions, or a sense of community, they are not feeling lucky.

- Don't try to hurry them along. They need time to reflect on the experience and take the time to recover.

- Unless you have had the identical experience, don't tell them you understand.

- Don't compare their loss to someone else's loss.

- Don't tell them other people's losses were worse than their loss.

- Don't tell them to be grateful for what they have.

- Don't tell them what they should have done differently.

HOW NOT TO SAY IT

At least you weren't hurt.

Be grateful it was just material things.

Be thankful you survived.

It could have been worse.

It wasn't that big a deal.

Many people were hurt worse.

Thankfully it only hit a small area.

SAMPLE LETTER/E-MAIL

To a friend whose home was destroyed in a tornado.

June X, 2XXX
Dear Karina:

I was stunned and scared to hear that a tornado had ripped through your town last night. When Diane finally heard from you, I was so relieved to know you, Ken, and the kids were okay, but I understand that, unbelievably, your entire house was demolished.

I am sending this to your mother's house because I know that's where you will be living for a while, but I want to extend an open invitation for you to stay with us for any length of time. In the meantime, I will plan on coming down as soon as the road is reopened to help with the cleanup effort and anything else you need.

I love you, and I am always here for you,
Annie

For further information:

Levy, Naomi. *To Begin Again—The Journey Toward Comfort, Strength, and Faith in Difficult Times.* New York, NY: Ballantine Books, 1998.

Matsakis, Aphrodite, Ph.D. *I Can't Get Over It: A Handbook for Trauma Survivors, Second Edition.* Oakland, CA: New Harbinger Publications, Inc., 1996.

American Red Cross National Headquarters
431 18th Street, NW
Washington, DC 20006
(202) 303-4498
www.redcross.org

Anxiety Disorders Association of America
8730 Georgia Avenue, Suite 600

Silver Spring, MD 20910

(240) 485-1001

www.adaa.org

Federal Emergency Management Agency (FEMA)

500 C Street, SW

Washington, DC 20472

(202) 566-1600

www.fema.gov

National Institute of Mental Health (NIMH)

6001 Executive Boulevard, Room 8184, MSC 9663

Bethesda, MD 20892-9663

(301) 443-4513 or toll-free (866) 615-NIMH

www.nimh.nih.gov

Salvation Army National Headquarters

615 Slaters Lane

P.O. Box 269

Alexandria, VA 22313

See also: WHAT IS GRIEF? UNDERSTANDING THE PROCESS OF MOURNING AND HOW CAN YOU HELP, WHAT CAN I SAY? COMMUNICATIONS THAT COMFORT, and WHAT CAN I DO? HOW TO LISTEN.

SEVENTEEN

Terrorism

*"In times like these, it helps to recall that there have
always been times like these."*

—Paul Harvey

THE unspeakable happened on September 11, 2001. It forever changed our
perception of safety and initiated feelings of vulnerability in the fragility
and unpredictability of life.

The events of September 11 were particularly personal and close to home,
but outrageous and shocking events occur in the world every day, leaving us
feeling powerless and with a sense of unreality. We are unprepared for the unexpected trauma resulting from terrorist violence. Those who experience the disasters firsthand are not the only ones affected; anyone who witnesses these events,
views the sites, or experiences loss, such as family members, emergency and res-
cue workers, medical and mental health professionals, and the entire nation, can
be impacted by the experience.

We are all vulnerable to trauma, even healthy and well-adjusted individuals.
It's important to understand that any experience with trauma can lead to long-
lasting problems.

If you suspect that someone you love is having difficulty recovering from
trauma or the symptoms seem especially severe and prolonged and you think
they might be experiencing post traumatic stress disorder (PTSD), you might
want to seek help from a professional—only a trained professional can make a
diagnosis of PTSD. If you are interested in exploring and learning more about
PTSD, see the resources at the end of this chapter.

The road to recovery from terrorist violence is a slow one. Your patient support and presence, both immediately following the event and in the years to
come, will go a long way in helping the survivor heal.

THINGS TO CONSIDER

- Terrorism can be a single act in which one person is hurt or killed or in which thousands are hurt and/or killed. What differentiates the magnitude of this trauma is the sheer numbers of dead and wounded; the impact of the death, destruction, and damage can be very overwhelming.

- Traumatic events can happen to anyone.

- No one can prepare for or protect themselves from a traumatic event.

- Survivors feel an overwhelming loss of control.

- Survivors will be forever influenced by their experience.

- Survivors report their reaction to trauma as feeling as if they are going crazy. They are not. They are experiencing symptoms and problems that are in response to the traumatic experience.

- Survivors can feel a tremendous sense of guilt and wonder why they survived and not others.

EMOTIONS AND FEELINGS TO ANTICIPATE

- Aggressiveness
- Anger
- Anxiety
- Blame
- Denial
- Despair
- Disbelief
- Disorientation
- Distress
- Fear
- Grief
- Guilt
- Helplessness
- Hopelessness
- Horror
- Humiliation
- Hurt
- Irritability
- Resentment
- Sadness
- Self-blame
- Shame
- Shock
- Terror
- Upset

WHAT TO SAY AND DO

- Extend your sympathy and let the survivor know that you care about them and their well-being.

- Be understanding.

- Let them know you are available to listen.

- Be patient; trauma survivors often speak slowly and haltingly while sharing their feelings and experiences.

- Reinforce that you believe them.

- Reassure them that it is normal to feel stressful reactions following a traumatic event.

- Encourage them to experience their feelings and fully grieve for their tragic loss.

- Affirm and believe all their personal responses and reactions to their experience and loss.

- Accept who they have become; trauma can change the survivors, and they need unconditional love to work through the healing process.

> ↷ Volunteer to provide transportation to support group meetings or offer to attend the meetings with them.

- Do learn as much as you can about trauma recovery and PTSD.

- Encourage the survivor to find support groups. It is important for them to relate to others who have been through the same or similar experiences.

- If they are unable to take the initiative, locate support groups for them.

- Invite the survivor to participate in physical exercise such as walking or swimming.

> ↷ Survivors might benefit from relaxation activities. Give them a gift certificate for a massage, a yoga or relaxation videotape, or suggest taking a class together that promotes relaxation.

- Recommend that they keep a journal of their thoughts and feelings.

- Let them know that it is okay to cry, and realize that it is okay for you to cry along with them.

- Suggest the survivor explore education and counseling to recover from the trauma.

- If the survivor is unable to do so, offer to research available support services for them.

HOW TO SAY IT

I am so grateful you survived.

I am so sorry this happened.

I love you, and I will be here for you.

I will be here for you no matter what, no matter when, because I love you and care about you.

I'm here for you.

You couldn't have known.

You did the best you could to protect yourself.

You handled yourself the best way you could under the circumstances.

WHAT NOT TO SAY AND DO

- Don't communicate lowered expectations to the survivor; if you do, they might think you feel they aren't capable or strong enough to overcome the traumatic event.

- Don't judge.

- Don't pressure or force someone to get help.

- Don't exhibit frustration if you feel they are not healing as quickly as you think they should.

- Don't tell them not to think about it.

- Don't tell them it is time to move on with their life.

HOW NOT TO SAY IT

Don't think about it.

It doesn't help to dwell on it.

It's time to move on with your life.

Just put it behind you.

Pretend it didn't happen.

Why can't you get over it, already?

SAMPLE LETTER/E-MAIL

To a friend who experienced a traumatic event.

October X, 2XXX
Dear Shawn:

I was so saddened to hear that you were injured and shocked to learn how it happened. Your sister shared that you will spend some time in rehabilitation while your injuries heal.

No one could possibly have predicted that this would happen, and I am grateful you survived. I have never experienced anything like this, and I find myself at a loss for what I can say that would bring you comfort.

You demonstrated tremendous courage, Shawn, in a very difficult situation. I respect your strength and tenacity and know that you did everything humanly possible to survive.

When you are up for some company, I would like to visit. In the meantime, I am sending positive thoughts your way. May you feel the warmth of the sun shine on you again soon.

Fondly,
Danielle

For further information:

To locate specialists or support groups for PTSD:

- The Sidran Foundation, (410) 825-8888.

- Anxiety Disorders Association of America, (212) 543-5355.

- American Psychological Association, (800) 964-2000.

- National Alliance for the Mentally Ill (NAMI), (800) 950-6264.

- Check in the Yellow Pages of your local telephone book pages for Mental Health Services.

Cart, Michael, ed., with Marc Aronson and Marianne Carus. *911—The Book of Help.* Chicago, IL: Cricket Books, 2002.

Doka, Kenneth J., ed., Ph.D. *Living with Grief After Sudden Loss: Suicide, Homicide, Accident, Heart Attack, Stroke.* Bristol, PA: Taylor & Francis, 1996.

Lattanzi-Licht, Marcia E., and Kenneth J. Doka, eds. *Living with Grief: Coping with Public Tragedy.* Washington, DC: Hospice Foundation of America, 2003.

Matsakis, Aphrodite, Ph.D. *I Can't Get Over It: A Handbook for Trauma Survivors, Second Edition.* Oakland, CA: New Harbinger Publications, Inc., 1996.

Wolfelt, Alan D., Ph.D. *Healing Your Traumatized Heart: 100 Practical Ideas After Someone You Love Dies a Sudden, Violent Death.* Fort Collins, CO: Companion Press, 2002.

American Red Cross National Headquarters
431 18th Street, NW
Washington, DC 20006
(202) 303-4498
www.redcross.org

Anxiety Disorders Association of America
8730 Georgia Avenue, Suite 600
Silver Spring, MD 20910
(240) 485-1001
www.adaa.org

Coping with Disaster
www.nmha.org/reassurance/anniversary/index.cfm

Coping with War and Terrorism: Tips for the Workplace
www.nmha.org/reassurance/workplaceWarCoping.cfm

Federal Emergency Management Agency (FEMA)
500 C Street, SW
Washington, DC 20472
(202) 566-1600
www.fema.gov

National Center for Victims of Crime
2000 M Street, NW, Suite 480
Washington, DC 20036
(202) 467-8700
www.ncvc.org

National Institute of Mental Health (NIMH)
6001 Executive Boulevard, Room 8184, MSC 9663
Bethesda, MD 20892-9663
(301) 443-4513 or toll-free (866) 615-NIMH
www.nimh.nih.gov

National Organization for Victim Assistance (NOVA)
1730 Park Road NW
Washington, DC 20010
(202) 232-6682
Information and referrals for victims of crime and disaster (800) TRY-NOVA
www.try-nova.org

The Salvation Army National Headquarters
615 Slaters Lane
P.O. Box 269
Alexandria, VA 22313
www.salvationarmyusa.org/www_usn.nsf

Especially for children:

Reactions and Guidelines for Children Following Trauma/Disaster

www.apa.org/practice/ptguidelines.html

Tragic Times Healing Words

www.sesameworkshop.org/parents/advice/article.php?contentId=49560#1

See also: WHAT IS GRIEF? UNDERSTANDING THE PROCESS OF MOURNING AND HOW YOU CAN HELP, WHAT CAN I SAY? COMMUNICATIONS THAT COMFORT, and WHAT CAN I DO? HOW TO LISTEN.

EIGHTEEN

Legal or Criminal Problems

*"You never know when a moment and a few sincere words
can have an impact on a life."*

—Zig Ziglar

Iт is shocking to open the daily newspaper and read that your neighbor's son has been arrested for drunk driving or a childhood friend's brother has been indicted for tax fraud. We know everyone is "innocent until proven guilty," but investigations, indictments, and arrests all raise the suspicion of guilt. Despite pleas of innocence, any conviction, fine, forfeiture of license, or incarceration carries a guilty stigma.

Anyone who experiences legal and/or criminal problems feels extreme shame, confusion, and fear; their problems shadow their loved ones, who experience the same emotions. Whether guilty or innocent, the experience is traumatizing— even more so if the news is broadcast locally or nationally in newspapers or on the radio or television.

Everyone reacts differently to these experiences, and it is impossible to predict how someone you care about will respond. They might desire seclusion or want your companionship or support.

Dealing with criminal or legal issues is both stressful and isolating. But if you are to continue the relationship, you can't ignore what has happened. Communications require great sensitivity, and the right words at the right time will demonstrate your support and keep the lines of communication open.

THINGS TO CONSIDER

- No one is prepared to deal with their own criminal or legal problems, even if they have a legal or criminal background.

- Individuals and their families who find themselves dealing with investigation, arrest, incarceration, or indictment need a great deal of information, resources, and support.

- Loved ones might experience severe financial hardship by hiring legal and investigative experts.

EMOTIONS AND FEELINGS TO ANTICIPATE

- Anger
- Denial
- Desire to flee
- Desperation
- Embarrassment

- Fear
- Guilt
- Loss
- Sadness
- Shame

WHAT TO SAY AND DO

- Let your family members, friends, or neighbors know that you are thinking of them and are sorry they are experiencing such a difficult situation.

- If they are uncomfortable speaking with you by telephone, communicate with them by notes and e-mail.

- If you don't get much of a response from them, continue to keep in touch, reinforcing again and again that you care about them.

- Offer to help in ways that are compatible with the type of relationship you have. For some, a note or phone call is sufficient; those with closer relationships can volunteer to research legal experts, provide meals, offer transportation, or volunteer to attend legal meetings, hearings, or court proceedings to extend support and take notes.

> ↻ Your loved ones might be embarrassed and prefer their privacy. With patience, they may be willing to resume their relationship with you.

- Be patient. Your loved ones might be overwhelmed with emotions they have never experienced, or they might be at a loss for how to deal with their feelings and the world at large.

HOW TO SAY IT

I am available for whatever you need me to do.

I am so sorry this is happening.

I have no idea what you might need, but I will help you in any way I can.

I know John is a fine person, and he will get through this.

I love you, and I will be there for you.

Know that you are often in my thoughts.

You are a wonderful person, and nothing can change that.

WHAT NOT TO SAY AND DO

- Don't ask for details of what happened. If someone wants to share detailed information with you, they will initiate the conversation themselves.

- Don't pressure them to talk to you.

- Don't pester them. If they won't take your calls or respond to your e-mail messages, they probably need privacy.

- Don't try to force them to see you by showing up uninvited or appearing in court or at a public venue.

- Don't break down when you see them, appearing as if you are the one who needs comfort.

HOW NOT TO SAY IT

How could he (she) do this?

How did this happen?

Is he (she) guilty?

Is it true?

It's in the newspaper; everyone is going to know.

How much is this all going to cost?

What is everyone going to think?

Special Situations

My cousin's son has been arrested for assault.
Send your cousin a note and let them know you are sorry this has happened. Remind them that you care about them and are ready to support them in any way. Refrain from making judgments or coming to any conclusions on the arrest charges. If your cousin would like to share any experiences with you, be there to listen. Do not give advice unless specifically asked to do so. The greatest gift you can give your cousin is to be there for them. Let them know what you are available to do, such as attend hearings with them, fix a meal, or just keep them company in the evening. If you receive no response from your outreach, continue to send notes or cards and keep in touch. This might be so difficult for your cousin that they are unable to respond to your efforts.

SAMPLE LETTERS/E-MAILS

To a friend whose son is under investigation for embezzlement.

> January X, 2XXX
> Dear Tom:
>
> You have frequently been in my thoughts. Having no experience in what you are going through, I am uncertain what to say or do to help you. Our friendship spans decades, and our children further cemented our relationship. It's been a pleasure to be part of Peter's life, and I am so terribly sorry this has happened. Please know that Beth and I think the world of you and your family. Nothing will change that.
>
> I will give you a call in a week or so to see how you are doing. I will be available to listen or support you in any way you'd like.
>
> Take good care of yourself.
> John

To a friend whose son is experiencing legal problems.

October X, 2XXX

Dear Carolyn:

Just sending a note to say hello. I really enjoyed getting together for lunch last month—let's do it again and see if Tara's available.

Carolyn, I can't say I know how you feel, but you are not alone. I know several people whose kids have been arrested—but you'll never know about it! Part of suburban (maybe "modern" would be a better description) life is maintaining the front that your own family is just fine, thank you. I think we'd all be better off dropping the charade and sharing more of what really goes on.

I just wanted you to know that I'm thinking of you and will help in any way. If you're looking for a good juvenile attorney, I can provide some names. I can write a reference for David, or if you just want to talk, give me a call or e-mail.

I've known David since our kids were in kindergarten together, and he is one fine young man, thanks to you and Ted. This experience might be unpleasant for everyone, but I'm confident he'll get through it and go on to college and a successful life.

So take care of yourself, and keep in touch.

Best,

JoAnn

For further information:

Bergman, Paul, and Sara J. Berman-Barrett. *The Criminal Law Handbook: Know Your Rights, Survive the System (Criminal Law Handbook, 5th Ed.).* Berkeley, CA: Nolo Press, 2003.

Feinman, Jay. *Law 101: Everything You Need to Know About the American Legal System.* Oxford, England: Oxford University Press, 2000.

Herskowitz, Suzan. *Legal Research Made Easy (Self-Help Law Kit).* Naperville, IL: Sourcebooks Trade, 1998.

Hill, Douglas J. *Federal Criminal Defendant's Handbook.* New York, NY: Kensington Publishers, 1999.

AllLaw.com
Find legal information or a lawyer in your geographic area.
www.AllLaw.com

American Bar Association
Extensive online source of legal information.
www.abanet.org

American Law Sources On-Line
Comprehensive, uniform, and useful compilation of links to freely accessible online sources of law for the United States and Canada.
www.lawsource.com

FindLaw.com
Research your legal questions online or search directly for a lawyer in your area.
www.findlaw.com

Nolo—Law for All
Nolo is the nation's leading provider of self-help legal books, software, and web-based information and tools.
www.nolo.com

See also: WHAT IS GRIEF? UNDERSTANDING THE PROCESS OF MOURNING AND HOW YOU CAN HELP, WHAT CAN I SAY? COMMUNICATIONS THAT COMFORT, and WHAT CAN I DO? HOW TO LISTEN.

COMMUNICATING ABOUT PERSONAL AND FAMILY ISSUES

Although change is inevitable, some of life's personal and family challenges are unanticipated, unwanted, or terribly disappointing. How individuals cope with personal and family losses and whether they move forward in their lives often depends on their network of support.

You can play a crucial role in helping your loved one, friend, co-worker, or community member recover from loss and disappointment.

Part Five provides specific insight into infertility, adoption, a baby or child with special needs, physical disability, separation, divorce, job loss, financial troubles, caregiver responsibilities, and personal disappointment, with guidelines on verbal, written, and nonverbal communications that you can use to comfort.

NINETEEN

Infertility

"One kind word can warm three winter nights."

—Asian saying

INFERTILITY, the inability to conceive a child, is a highly personal medical condition that can be emotionally devastating to the couple trying to start a family. The National Center for Health Statistics reports infertility affects 6.1 million Americans—approximately one in six couples.

To women who were lectured in their early teens to avoid the risk of pregnancy, it is a cruel irony that when they are ready to take on the responsibility and role of parenthood, they can't. It is incredibly frustrating to reach the status of an adult and find you have no control over your fertility.

Many women feel an overwhelming sense of failure and wonder "Why me?" Why are they being singled out when it seems like everyone else can get pregnant whether they want to or not? Women are not alone in their feelings of failure and frustration; infertility is a real blow to the male ego. Many men are demoralized when undergoing infertility testing, and they might feel their masculinity threatened if the results indicate problems with their sperm.

Medical professionals can provide details of the physical and physiological barriers that prevent pregnancy, but there are no known psychological barriers. Well-meaning family members and friends often suggest behavioral adjustments, but there is no proof that an optimistic outlook, how hard the couple try or don't try, or their degree of relaxation has any impact on the likelihood of achieving gestation.

Modern medicine has made significant breakthroughs in helping infertile couples achieve pregnancy. Technology continues to provide new opportunities, which lead to innovative options for individuals and partners to have children.

It is important to understand that although many of these options have helped individuals and partners have children, they can be expensive, painful, complicated, not in line with someone's religious beliefs, or just not feasible for the individuals or couples. Some of them are just too high a price to pay to become pregnant, and none of them are guaranteed.

Parents, siblings, grandparents, and other relatives, in their love and desire to expand the family, have the capacity to exacerbate an already stressful situation. In-laws should be particularly sensitive in broaching the subject of fertility.

Infertility is a sensitive topic, and if not handled well, you can easily cause a serious strain or rift in the relationship between you and the individual or partner. Communications require diplomacy and tact, and your caring support will help them work through this difficult and frustrating experience.

THINGS TO CONSIDER

- Infertility does not discriminate—it strikes all income levels and all races.

- The inability to conceive is a deeply personal experience.

- The relationship you have with the individual or partner.

- Did you have difficulty getting pregnant?

- Do you have children? If so, are they biological or adopted?

- Moods and emotions may be erratic as a result of infertility medications.

EMOTIONS AND FEELINGS TO ANTICIPATE

- Anger
- Anxiousness
- Confusion
- Depression
- Desperation
- Embarrassment
- Failure
- Frustration
- Guilt
- Isolation
- Jealousy
- Longing
- Misery
- Obsessiveness
- Sadness
- Vulnerability

WHAT TO SAY AND DO

■ Do be understanding and supportive.

■ Do make yourself available to listen. If the individual shares his or her feelings, be empathetic.

■ Do be thoughtful if continued infertility is causing stress and depression. Lift their spirits with movie tickets for two, a gift certificate to a spa, or a CD from their favorite artist.

> ↜ You can demonstrate support if they are going through medical procedures by offering to take them to physician appointments or bringing dinner the night of a procedure.

■ Do understand if the couple is sensitive or uncomfortable in attending baby showers or family events that focus on pregnancy and babies.

■ Do offer the couple the opportunity to attend an event late or leave early so they can make a quick "cameo" appearance.

■ Do understand if they choose not to attend.

HOW TO SAY IT

Go ahead and cry; I'll stay with you.

How would you like me to be there for you?

I would like to support you; please let me know how I can be there for you.

If you need me, I am here for you.

It must be hard to go through this.

There is always hope.

What can I do that will help you?

You can talk to me; I care.

WHAT NOT TO SAY AND DO

- Don't ask a childless couple "When do you plan to have children?"

- Don't initiate conversations on infertility; always take your cues from the couple.

- Don't downplay the problem by telling them "At least you have each other and your health" or "Thank goodness you already have a child."

- Don't give any unsolicited advice on how to get pregnant or recommendations of unproven techniques such as herbal remedies or sexual timing.

- Don't tell them to relax or suggest their intense focus on pregnancy is causing them unnecessary stress.

- Don't tell personal stories about your own fertility, such as "I got pregnant both times I tried."

- Don't second-guess their physician by telling them medical techniques to pursue; assume they have conducted research and are using a competent medical professional.

- Don't blame them for their infertility.

- Don't tell them anything that might make them feel guilty, such as "You should have tried sooner."

- Don't pressure a woman to attend any event that makes her feel uncomfortable and is a reminder that she is not pregnant.

- Don't share stories about other couples who either failed to become pregnant or who successfully became pregnant; these stories won't make them feel better.

- Don't express negative opinions on fertility treatments and adoption; these might be their best alternatives to have a child.

HOW NOT TO SAY IT

All I have to do is look at my husband and I get pregnant.

Don't be so blue.

Go away for a romantic weekend.

My friend adopted a baby, and she got pregnant right away.

Take a cruise.

When are you going to have your next one?

Whose fault is it you can't get pregnant?

You are trying too hard.

You need to relax.

Special Situations

It took my cousin years before she was able to conceive, and her daughter is now five years old. I think she might be experiencing infertility again and I would like to be supportive.
She might have made the choice to have an only child. Or she might be experiencing secondary infertility. She has not mentioned anything to you about the subject, so I would keep quiet. She will initiate a conversation if and when she wants to discuss this with you.

My co-worker has completed her third attempt at in vitro fertilization, and this last attempt failed like the others.
Your co-worker is terribly disappointed and needs your support. This is not the time to give advice or opinions concerning fertility methods or even adoption. She and her partner need to make their own decision on what path to choose. Let her know that you care about her and will support whatever decision she makes. The decision to pursue further fertility treatments is a decision only your friend and her partner can make.

SAMPLE LETTER/E-MAIL

To a friend who has just confided that she has been unable to conceive.

> January X, 2XXX
> Dear Elizabeth:
>
> My thoughts have been with you all morning. Thank you so much for sharing your feelings and experiences with me yesterday.
> Now I understand better how difficult this has been for you and Bill. I will be here for you in any way I can. Know that I am praying that things will work out and your dreams will come true. You are always in my heart.
>
> Love,
> Kate

For further information:

Domar, Alice D., Ph.D., and Alice Lesch Kelly. *Conquering Infertility: Dr. Alice Domar's Mind/Body Guide to Enhancing Fertility and Coping with Infertility.* New York, NY: Viking Press, 2002.

Indichova, Julia. *Inconceivable: A Woman's Triumph over Despair and Statistics.* New York, NY: Broadway Books, 2001.

Marrs, Richard, M.D., Lisa Friedman Bloch, and Kathy Kirtland Silverman, *Dr. Richard Marrs' Fertility Book: America's Leading Infertility Expert Tells You Everything You Need to Know About Getting Pregnant.* New York, NY: Dell Books, 1998.

The Staff of *Resolve* and Diane Aronson. *Resolving Infertility.* New York, NY: HarperCollins Publishers, 2001.

Zouves, Christo, and Julie Sullivan, cont. *Expecting Miracles: On the Path of Hope from Infertility to Parenthood.* New York, NY: Henry Holt & Company, 1999.

American Society for Reproductive Medicine
(Formerly The American Fertility Society)
1209 Montgomery Highway
Birmingham, AL 35216-2809
(205) 978-5000
www.asrm.org

CDC's Reproductive Health Information Source
Division of Reproductive Health
National Center for Chronic Disease Prevention and Health Promotion
Centers for Disease Control and Prevention
4770 Buford Highway, NE, Mail Stop K-20
Atlanta, GA 30341-3717
(770) 488-5200

MEDLINE plus Health Information—Infertility
A Service of the U.S. National Library of Medicine and the National Institutes of Health
www.nlm.nih.gov/medlineplus/infertility.html

RESOLVE, Inc.
National Headquarters
1310 Broadway
Somerville, MA 02144
(888) 623-0744
www.resolve.org

See also: WHAT IS GRIEF? UNDERSTANDING THE PROCESS OF MOURNING AND HOW YOU CAN HELP, WHAT CAN I SAY? COMMUNICATIONS THAT COMFORT, and WHAT CAN I DO? HOW TO LISTEN.

TWENTY

Adoption

"An 'adoptive parent' is a special kind of person.
Not just any grown-up can be one."

—Carole Livingston, *Why Was I Adopted?*

As parents of adopted children will tell you, adoption is just another way to form a family. Individuals and couples choose adoption for a variety of reasons, but primarily because they want to love and share their life with a child and raise that child as their own.

Married couples might choose to adopt because they can't have a child together, or because they already have a child and want to give another child a home and a family. Single adults might choose to adopt because they want to be a parent and feel they can raise a child on their own. In stepfamilies, a stepparent can adopt the child or children of their spouse. And in some instances, a family member adopts a child who was parented by another family member.

The joys and challenges of parenting are the same for adoptive families as they are for biological families. Approximately 120,000 children are adopted annually, and the number has remained consistent through the last decade. Slightly less than half of all adoptions are *related adoptions,* meaning children were adopted by stepparents or other family members.

Chances are that you know someone who is adopted. About 1.5 million children in the United States reside with adoptive parents—approximately 2 percent of all children age eighteen and under. More than 7 million adopted individuals of all ages live in the United States.

A survey conducted by the Adoption Institute found that 60 percent of Americans have had a personal experience with adoption; either they or a family member or close friend was adopted, they themselves had adopted, or they had placed a child for adoption. Approximately one third of the country—close to 100 million Americans—has adoption within their immediate family.

Parents have begun looking to other countries to adopt healthy babies and children. Between the years 1971 and 2001, 265,677 children from other countries were adopted by U.S. citizens. International adoptions have more than doubled in the last eleven years, from 9,000 in 1991 to 20,099 in 2002.

The U.S. State Department reported that more children were adopted from abroad in 2002 than in any year since records were kept. China led all countries for the third consecutive year in U.S. adoptions; the top eight countries include China, 5,053; Russia, 4,939; Guatemala, 2,219; South Korea, 1,779; Ukraine, 1,106; Kazakhstan, 819; Vietnam, 766; and India, 466.

A new family addition is a time for joy, but a period of adjustment follows the excitement. They will need your help and support during this transitional period.

THINGS TO CONSIDER

- Adoption is another way to be a family; adopting or being adopted is just different, not second-best.

- Insensitive attention or questions, no matter how well intentioned, can hurt adopted children, their siblings, and their parents.

- Families who adopt a child from a foreign country do so to build a family; the adopted children become their "own" children.

EMOTIONS AND FEELINGS TO ANTICIPATE

- Anxiety
- Apprehensiveness
- Excitement
- Fear
- Gratefulness
- Happiness
- Joy
- Nervousness
- Relief
- Uncertainty
- Vulnerability

WHAT TO SAY AND DO

- Congratulate the parent(s).

- Just as you might inquire about the due date of an expectant mother, it's okay to ask prospective adoptive parents if they have information about the arrival, such as "Do you have any idea when this will happen?"

- If you know someone who has adopted children from the same type of agency or the same country, you can ask "Would you like to meet another international family?" or "Would you like to know another family who adopted privately?" But don't be offended if the parent(s) don't accept your offer; it is a period of vulnerability that leaves the parent(s) exhilarated but emotionally drained while waiting for a child to be offered and waiting for the child to arrive. The parent(s) might wish to keep this time private.

> ☞ If the adoption requirements necessitate the family traveling to and possibly staying in a foreign country to await the adoption, ask what you can do for them while they are away. You can take care of the mail, the newspaper, watering the plants, or any other household chores.

- Familiarize yourself with the adoption process so you will understand how the adoption is proceeding, how you can help, and what it's all about.

- Send flowers if that's what you would do for the birth of a baby.

- Write cards and notes of congratulations.

- Choose a gift appropriate for the child's age.

> ☞ Be specific in asking how you can help. Letters of recommendation may be part of the adoption process, and you can offer to write a letter on their behalf. If photographs are required, you can offer to take and print the photographs.

- Offer to bring lunch or a dinner.

- Do refer to the child as their daughter or their son; avoid describing them as their "adopted daughter" or "adopted son."

- If the parent(s) adopt a child from another race, be sensitive in your comments.

- Do approach the family with kindness and accept them as a family. Avoid asking any questions that make the parents and children feel uncomfortable. Parents and children want to be accepted for what they are—a family—and they do not enjoy being questioned about personal matters.

HOW TO SAY IT

How are you feeling?

How can I help?

How exciting!

I am so happy for you!

I can't wait to meet him (her).

That's terrific!

This is great!

What can I do to help?

What lucky parents to have such a wonderful child.

What wonderful news!

> ↷ Before you say anything to a parent of an adopted child, ask yourself if this is appropriate commentary for a parent of a biological child. If you would say the same thing to a parent of a biological child, then it is probably appropriate to say to a parent of an adopted child.

WHAT NOT TO SAY AND DO

- Don't imply that an adopted child is not quite as good or is second-best to a biological child.

- Don't relate horror stories that you might have heard about adoption in general or adoption from a particular country or source; rest assured that the parent(s) have investigated and weighed all sources of information.

- Don't ask intimate questions about the child's history, such as "So what is the story with the birthparents?" or "Was he (she) abandoned?"

- Don't ask questions on any facet of the adoption or their child's heritage in front of the child.

- Avoid comments that imply the parents "saved" the child they adopted. In that same vein, don't describe the parents as selfless or saints; they adopted this child because they wanted to be a family.

- Don't express negative opinions or your personal concerns about adoption.

- There are certain ways of referring to adoptive family members that you should avoid; don't refer to the child's birth parents as the "real parents," and don't refer to the child that is adopted as an "orphan" or as an "unwanted" child.

> ✎ Outdated language needs to be replaced with a more modern vocabulary that will protect an adopted child's privacy and preserve their self-esteem. The "parents" are the parents who are raising the child and the "birth parents" are the child's biological parents.

- Don't suggest friends or family members who are interested in adoption call someone you know who is in the process of adopting. Individuals going through the adoption process are dealing with many emotions and fears, and it is important to respect their privacy during the adoption process.

- Many children experience problems during different phases of their development. If someone's adopted child is having difficulty, don't inquire "Do you think that behavior is related to their adoption?"

- Do not ask parents of young international children if their child has characteristics of the parent country, such as "Does your child speak Korean?" or "Is he a Communist?"

HOW NOT TO SAY IT

Are they real sisters?

Are those kids really yours?

Aren't you nice for doing that.

Can you love this child as much as you would your own?

Can't you have a child of your own?

Do you have children of your own?

Do your kids know they are adopted?

How could the real mother give him (her) away?

How much did it cost?

How much did you pay for the child?

Is she yours?

What happens if you have natural children?

Why did you do that?

You are doing these kids such a favor.

NONVERBAL STRATEGIES

Sometimes, the parents have little notice that a child is available. In some cases, the parents might not be ready for the child, and there are a number of things you can do to help out.

- Offer to purchase the basic necessities such as diapers, wipes, bottles, formula, baby food, and other sundry items.

- Volunteer to arrange or pick up furniture for the nursery or to help set up the nursery.

- Offer to loan the prospective parents equipment such as a stroller, car seat, high chair, or age-appropriate clothing.

Special Situations

My friend's adoption fell through.
This is a painfully disappointing experience. Call your friend and tell them how sorry you are. If they are not accepting phone calls, write a note. Let them know that you care and will be there for them however they might need you. Offer to visit and be willing to sit with them and listen. Avoid telling them there will be

another chance and another child; they need to grieve for the child they have already taken into their hearts.

My friend and her husband entered into a private adoption. They had the baby for three weeks and then the birth mother changed her mind and took custody of the baby.

Your friend and her husband are devastated. They loved this baby, and they will need to grieve for their loss. Treat this situation like you would a death, with the same thoughtfulness, compassion, and kindness. Your friends will need time and patience to heal from this experience.

My friend adopted a child from Russia, and the child has health problems that require several surgeries.

Your friend is feeling blessed to have this child, and you should focus your efforts on welcoming and celebrating this new addition to the family. Offer your congratulations and emphasize the joy this child brings, responding in the same way you do for any new baby. You can send a card or a gift, bring a meal, or do something special for your friend. Your friend is not looking for sympathy, but he or she could probably use some help when the child is hospitalized. Be specific in offering help—volunteer to do some grocery shopping, bring a meal, provide child care or carpooling (if there is a sibling), and run errands.

SAMPLE LETTERS/E-MAILS

From an acquaintance, a gift of an Asian baby doll in a traditional red dress, in celebration of the adoption of a baby daughter born in Korea.

October X, 2XXX
Dear Margaret and John:

Red is the color of joy and happiness according to Eastern culture. The birth of a baby is celebrated by passing out red-dyed eggs, and the newborn is dressed in red. I know Suzanne has brought you much joy and will continue to do so. Congratulations! I hope she will enjoy this doll.

Fondly,
Debbie, Bill, Lisa, and Hillary

From a family friend on the adoption of a son.

> May X, 2XXX
> Dear Maggie and Griffin:
>
> Just got a call from Charlie Jones with the good news of your baby son, Jason. So very delighted for you both—and, of course, our wishes for a wonderful life together always.
>
> I am sure you are both thrilled and Jason is blessed to have such terrific parents. Please give him a big kiss for us.
>
> Much love,
> Dorothy and Jack

For additional information:

Adamec, Chris. *The Complete Idiot's Guide to Adoption.* Indianapolis, IN: Alpha Books, 1998.

Johnston, Patricia Irwin. *Adopting After Infertility.* Indianapolis, IN: Perspectives Press, 1996.

Register, Cherie. *Are Those Kids Yours?* New York, NY: Free Press, 1990.

Van Gulden, Holly, and Lisa M. Bartels-Rabb. *Real Parents, Real Children: Parenting the Adopted Child.* New York, NY: Crossroad, 1995.

The National Adoption Center
1500 Walnut Street, Suite 701
Philadelphia, PA 19102
(800) TO-ADOPT
www.adopting.org

National Adoption Center's Learning Center offers a variety of online adoption education, information, and support services.
www.adoptnet.org

For comprehensive resources on all aspects of adoption:
The National Adoption Information Clearinghouse
330 C Street SW
Washington, DC 20447

(703) 352-3488 or (888) 251-0075
www.naic.acf.hhs.gov/index.cfm

RESOLVE, Inc.
National Headquarters
1310 Broadway
Somerville, MA 02144
(888) 623-0744
www.resolve.org

Especially for children:

Krementz, Jill. *How It Feels to Be Adopted.* New York, NY: Alfred A. Knopf, 1988.

Livingston, Carole. *Why Was I Adopted?* New York, NY: Carol Publishing Group, 1997.

Watkins, Mary, and Susan Fisher. *Talking with Young Children About Adoption.* New Haven, CT: Yale University Press, 1995.

TWENTY-ONE

Baby or Child with Special Needs

*"Friends in your life are like pillars on your porch. Sometimes
they hold you up, and sometimes they lean on you. Sometimes it's just
enough to know they're standing by."*

—Anonymous

MOST of us go into parenthood with great expectations; we long to share our love with our offspring and nurture them through a healthy and happy childhood. But this dream is not always a reality. It can be devastating for parents to learn that their dearly anticipated baby or child may be disabled and require a lifetime of special care.

The Maternal and Child Health Bureau estimates that 18 million children in the United States have "special health needs." And although these babies and children are special and beloved, the challenges to parenting can be exhausting and overwhelming.

Children with special health needs are defined as all children who have, or are at increased risk for, chronic physical, developmental, behavioral, or emotional challenges. These children will require health and related services of a type or amount beyond the normal requirements of children.

Approximately 18 percent of children have significant chronic conditions, and they consume 60 to 70 percent of the health-care resources spent on children. Examples of chronic conditions include asthma, cancer, autism, cerebral palsy, depression, and complications of prematurity. Care for these children requires coordination between primary and specialty health-care systems, schools, child care, early intervention programs, and community services.

Parenting the special needs child offers many rewards, but parents must first acknowledge that their dreams might be altered, postponed, or no longer possible. They might grieve for what they will not have the opportunity to experience—the typical childhood that might never be and the life that might be very different than the one they envisioned. They must work through this grief while dealing with difficult issues as they strive to ensure appropriate medical and developmental services for their child.

While raising a child with special needs is not the life the parent(s) dreamed, this different life will provide ample opportunities for childhood achievements. You can help support them by remaining a consistent presence in their lives. They will continue to need assistance and companionship throughout their child's life.

THINGS TO CONSIDER

- Parent(s) will spend a tremendous amount of time and energy mapping out diagnostic plans and new life, educational, and medical goals.

- Parent(s) will be sleep deprived, but especially so in the first year.

- Parent(s) might be severely impaired in maintaining almost any segment of their lives.

- The parents' relationship will meet unremitting stress and test every aspect of their relationships.

- Friends will need to understand that the difficult constraints will shift the balance of the relationship. The parent(s) will want and need to continue the friendship, but friends will need to expend 75 percent of the initiative with the parent(s) expending the other 25 percent.

- The parents' financial resources might be stretched to a point that previous expected and/or typical expenditures may end up being delayed, postponed, or eliminated.

- Parents will experience tremendous fear for what the future holds, the unknown parameters of the parents' altered life, and what will happen to the child when the parents die.

- Despite the inherent stresses, there will be pride and joy at different milestones, and even the simplest accomplishments are a cause for rejoicing.

EMOTIONS AND FEELINGS TO ANTICIPATE

- Anger
- Anxiety
- Fear
- Grief
- Happiness
- Hurt
- Jealousy

- Joy
- Love
- Pride
- Regret
- Resentment
- Sadness

WHAT TO SAY AND DO

- Do call rather than write a note; parents feel isolated, and they might falsely assume you are uncomfortable and avoiding them if you chose to write rather than call.

- Express your love for the child now and in the future.

- Do encourage the parent(s) to get a second opinion.

- Do let the parent(s) know it is okay to challenge the diagnosis and the doctor.

- Do let the parent(s) know it is okay to change doctors if the relationship is not working, and it is okay to get professional health-care assistance.

- Do ease any guilt by making them aware that what works for one family doesn't work for every family.

- Do bring a meal.

- Ask questions about the child's progress on a regular basis.

> ꙮ Solicit a sign-up sheet to deliver meals from members of the neighborhood, congregants, parents and faculty at the school, and any other club, institution, business, or organization that has a relationship with the family.

- Do take your cues and talk if they would like or be quiet together if they do not choose to talk.

- Encourage your relationship and a dialogue.

- Be persistent; the parent(s) might be insecure or uncomfortable participating in social activities and events, but keep asking.

- Engage any related faith-based organization for all types of support.

> ↪ Include siblings in activities and special events so they won't get lost in the shuffle.

- Ease the stress by offering to partner in any form of exercise; it is always easier to stay on an exercise regimen if someone is there to keep you on track.

- Offer to come to the house, answer the phone, and maintain some order while they take a nap.

- Understand and respect the necessary and existing boundaries.

- Share and take pride in the child's accomplishments.

- Encourage hobbies and special interests by ordering them a gift subscription to a hobby magazine or gift certificate to a hobby or craft store for a hobby or special interest they either enjoy or would like to pursue.

- If siblings are not in a support group, find information for them on local groups available for their special needs.

- Recommend that parents communicate with their police department and fire department that there is a child with special needs in the home.

- Suggest the child wear an identification bracelet should he (she) become separated from the caregiver.

- Do understand that holidays are especially stressful; they alter routines, and routines are necessary for a child with special needs.

- Do ask what you can do to make holidays less stressful.

- Do offer to do the traveling during holidays and try to accommodate the family in any way you can.

HOW TO SAY IT

Give yourself some time.

I don't know what you are going through, but you are in my heart and prayers.

I have a few free hours; can I come over and do (laundry, grocery shopping, etc.)?

It's okay to hope for more.

This is really hard.

This must be really rough for you.

We love you all; nothing will change that.

WHAT NOT TO SAY AND DO

- Don't ignore the family.

- Don't pretend it hasn't happened or act as if nothing is wrong; avoid comments such as "He'll grow out of it" or "I think she is just fine."

- Don't put a label on the child.

- Don't assume that you know the child's status and medical condition.

- Don't take it personally if your invitations are refused.

- Don't let them think they have to reinvent the wheel; encourage them or help them find out what has worked for other parents.

- Don't force conversation; it is okay for the parent(s) not to talk about it.

- Don't second-guess their parenting skills with comments such as "You are not strict enough" or "Don't you think you are being too overprotective?"

HOW NOT TO SAY IT

God will only give you what you can handle.

He (she) can't talk because he has nothing to say.

What do I tell the family?

What kind of life will he (she) have?

When will he (she) be normal?

Will he (she) ever go to school?

Will she (he) need to be institutionalized?

NONVERBAL STRATEGIES

- Offer to go grocery shopping or locate information on grocery delivery services.

- Volunteer to do the laundry.

- Ask for a list of errands to do while running your own.

- Offer to stay in the home while the child is sleeping so the parent can get some relief or run some errands.

- Provide help in researching physicians, medical facilities, articles, and other resources.

- Make a list of who they should be contacting, and locate the contacts for them.

- Help them find appropriate support groups; attend in their place to collect information or, if they are available to attend, go with them for support.

- Locate qualified respite care so they will have backup help and a breather from caregiver responsibilities.

- Do offer to care for another child or children in the family.

- Offer a gift certificate for a cleaning service.

- Provide transportation to medical appointments.

- Accompany the parent(s) to medical appointments; either watch the child while they are getting information or volunteer to take notes; they might not be able to process all the information.

- Encourage them to keep specific milestone, goal, medical, and prescription records.

- Offer to help organize their records or establish a system.

- Suggest maintaining a journal on all the physicians they have seen.

Special Situations

A friend and I had our babies around the same time, and the children played frequently. Her son has recently been diagnosed with autism.
Be persistent in retaining the relationship with your friend, but be aware that your child's milestones might cause her pain. Continue to invite her to outings, but don't be upset if she declines. You might have to work hard to find one special thing that is a successful experience for everyone such as an outing or activity whose physical requirements meet the child's special needs. It will be well worth the effort to preserve your relationship while your child learns appropriate ways to treat another person whose needs and life experience differ from his (her) own.

My cousin has a typically developing child and a child with special needs. Must both children be invited to birthday parties?
Invite both children and let your cousin know that she is welcome to come late or leave early to meet her special child's needs. It would be appropriate for another family member to volunteer to pick up or take home her other child so they can enjoy the full party. If the child with special needs is disruptive and your cousin allows the child to spoil the event, you can extend just one invitation to the nondisruptive child.

My friend has a child with special needs who enjoys going out to dinner. We join them for dinner out once a month, but occasionally an incident occurs involving the child and the adult friend is reprimanded by another adult in public.
Don't let the incident destroy your evening out. I bet your friend has lots of experience dealing with and diffusing these situations. Let her (him) know that the incident was awful; you are sorry it happened, but they handled it well. Be empathetic and let them know that you think they are doing a great job. You need to

be supportive of your friend, and if you are uncomfortable in these situations, find another way to spend time together.

For further information:

Klein, Stanley D., Ph.D., and Kim Schive, eds. *You Will Dream New Dreams: Inspiring Personal Stories by Parents of Children with Disabilities.* New York, NY: Kensington Publishing Corporation, 2001.

Lavin, Judith Loseff. *Special Kids Need Special Parents: A Resource for Parents of Children with Special Needs.* New York, NY: Berkley Publishing Group, 2001.

Morel, Janet. *Playing the Hand That's Dealt to You: A Guide for Parents of Children with Special Needs.* Melbourne Beach, FL: Canmore Press, 2000.

Naseef, Robert A. *Special Children, Challenged Parents: The Struggles and Rewards of Raising a Child with a Disability.* Baltimore, MD: Paul H. Brookes Publishing Company, 2001.

National Network for Childcare
www.nncc.org

Parenting Special Needs
specialchildren.about.com

Woodbine House
Publishers of the special-needs collection
www.woodbinehouse.com

See also: WHAT IS GRIEF? UNDERSTANDING THE PROCESS OF MOURNING AND HOW YOU CAN HELP, WHAT CAN I SAY? COMMUNICATIONS THAT COMFORT, and WHAT CAN I DO? HOW TO LISTEN.

TWENTY-TWO

Physical Disability

"People seldom refuse help, if one offers it in the right way."

—A. C. Benson

MANY people feel apprehensive when it comes to interacting with individuals with physical disabilities. Apprehension is rooted in fear, and it could be that we experience fear in not knowing what to say or do when we encounter someone with a physical disability. Or it might be that persons with disabilities are poignant reminders of life's fragilities. We might fear that we could easily be disabled, too.

Current statistics indicate that approximately 54 million Americans—about one in five—have a disability that interferes with their life activities. Disabilities are expected to impact 50 percent of the population by 2010.

Physical disability is defined by the Americans with Disabilities Act (ADA) as a person who has a physical or mental impairment that substantially limits one or more major life activities. The U.S. Census breaks disability into two categories—sensory disability, which includes blindness, deafness, or severe vision or hearing impairment; and physical disability, which includes a condition that substantially limits one or more basic physical activities such as walking, climbing stairs, reaching, lifting, or carrying.

Modern science has improved the quality and longevity of life for those with disabilities, and assistive technology and services have facilitated and enhanced independent living.

A disability can alter or change a person's life, but it doesn't necessarily change the person. You can help support individuals with disabilities by treating them with the same respect and reverence you use for anyone.

THINGS TO CONSIDER

- Some individuals might have genetic disabilities, while others might have become disabled later in life.

- Individuals with disabilities are each unique; they will have diverse skills, abilities, interests, and personalities.

- Individuals with disabilities are like everyone else; they possess the same feelings and emotions as other individuals.

- Individuals might not view their disability as a liability.

EMOTIONS AND FEELINGS TO ANTICIPATE

- Adaptable
- Anger
- Denial
- Despair
- Depression
- Determination
- Fear
- Focused
- Isolation
- Loneliness
- Loss
- Motivated
- Persuasive
- Sadness
- Sensitivity

WHAT TO SAY AND DO

- Relax and behave as you would in any social situation.

- Do communicate in ways that demonstrate respect for the individual's dignity.

- Do give them the freedom to interact and participate in any activity they choose.

- Do use positive rather than negative terms when referring to the individual's abilities; use "She walks with a walker" rather than "She cannot navigate without a walker."

- Do treat the individual the same way you would like to be treated.

- Do take your cues from the individual; if you offer help and they refuse, accept the refusal. If you offer help and they accept, allow them to instruct you how you can best help them.

- If they use an assistive device such as a wheelchair, crutches, a cane, or a walker, ask how you could help them. Do ensure that pathways are clear and accessible for easier access.

- Be specific when asking how you can accommodate them.

- Do let them know the dimensions of doorways and if doorways and entrances to restrooms are accessible. Do give them advance warning if there will be a problem with logistics.

> ☞ Always consider an alternative, inclusive location.

- Do treat them in the same way you would have treated them before; even if it is awkward to hug them, do so if you hugged them before.

- Speak to them at eye level if you will be speaking for any duration; either sit down on a seat or squat.

> ☞ If you are going to have an ongoing relationship with this individual, you will need to learn personal information about each other. It's okay to express genuine personal interest; it's not okay to inquire just because you are curious.

- Do take your cues from the individual in inquiring about their disability. Some individuals are comfortable in discussing it; others are not.

CHOOSE WORDS WITH DIGNITY

Basic Guidelines:

Make reference to the person first, then the disability, for example "A person with a disability" rather than "a disabled person."

The following words are affirmative and reflect a positive attitude.

The following words have strong negative connotations.

Words with Dignity	Do Not Use
Disability	Handicap
Person who has multiple sclerosis	Stricken with multiple sclerosis
Paraplegic (person with limited or no use of lower limbs)	Para
Quadriplegic (person with limited or no use of all four limbs)	Quad
Person who has cerebral palsy	Spastic
Person who has a speech impairment	Speech defect
Person with a head injury	The head injured
Person with AIDS	AIDS victim
Person who has polio, arthritis, etc.	Crippled with polio, arthritis, etc.
Person with mental retardation	Retard
Person with learning disability	Dim witted, slow

Words with Dignity	Do Not Use
Person with a mental disorder	Mentally ill
Person with an emotional disorder	Crazy
Person who is blind, partially blind	Blind guys, visually impaired*
Person who is deaf	Deaf and dumb, deaf mute
Person who is hard of hearing	Hearing impaired*
Sign language interpreter	Deaf interpreter
Born with "_____"	Birth defect
Caused by "_____"	Afflicted by
Nondisabled (referring to nondisabled persons as normal insinuates that disabled persons are not normal)	Normal
Person in a wheelchair	Confined/restricted to a wheelchair**
Person who walks with crutches, a walker, a cane, a limp, etc.	Crippled

*Many blind persons and deaf persons consider the words *visually impaired* and *hearing impaired* offensive. *Blind* simply means without the sense or use of sight. *Deaf* simply means partially or totally unable to hear. They believe these two words describe their situation best. They do not wish to be identified as diminished in strength or value, as the word *impaired* denotes.

**Crutches, walkers, and wheelchairs are mobility aids. Without the use of these mobility aids, the person might be restricted from participation in their community.

Used with permission from Iowa Department of Human Rights, Division of Persons with Disabilities, Des Moines, Iowa.

HOW TO SAY IT

How can I be most helpful?

Please let me know what would make you most comfortable.

What do I need to know about to accommodate your wheelchair?

WHAT NOT TO SAY AND DO

- Don't say a visit or a location will be okay if there are obstacles; let them know up front.

- Don't express pity when speaking to the individual.

- Don't avoid making eye contact or speaking without looking at them.

- Don't touch him or her without permission.

- Don't automatically push their wheelchair or take their arm.

- Avoid asking intimate questions that you would not ask an able-bodied person, such as "How do you eat?" or "How do you use the restroom?"

> ‍ Before you say anything to a person with a disability, ask yourself if this is appropriate commentary for an able-bodied person. If you would say the same thing to an able-bodied person, then it is probably appropriate to say to a person with a disability.

HOW NOT TO SAY IT

Do you mind telling me what happened?

How long have you been handicapped?

I am really amazed at how well you do.

It must be tough to have to use a walker.

It's unfortunate that you are confined to a wheelchair.

You should really be proud of yourself.

Special Situations

I would like to meet a new friend for lunch at a restaurant. He is in a wheelchair, and I want to make it comfortable for him.

Ask your friend whether he prefers sitting in his wheelchair or a regular chair. When you call to make a reservation, let them know that your friend is in a wheelchair and his preferences so they can accommodate you. If they don't take reservations, find out what time you should arrive to limit your wait. Ensure the logistics match your friend's needs, and inquire whether their restroom facilities can accommodate a wheelchair. Ask your friend for any other logistical information to ensure the experience is a good one.

My friend is hard of hearing, and I am unsure how to best communicate.

It's important to speak directly to your friend, as people who are hard of hearing may read lips. Ensure that you continue to look directly at him during your conversation, and avoid walking away while speaking. Understand that you might need to repeat your information; do so in a respectful manner without raising your voice.

SAMPLE LETTERS/E-MAILS

To an uncle who recently had a stroke.

> January X, 2XXX
> Dear Uncle Phil:
>
> Mary has been calling to keep me updated on your progress. I can only imagine how difficult this is for you. Everyone in the family has always said you were the one to tap for the toughest jobs. Little did we know how tough the jobs would become. I know in my heart that if anyone can surmount this challenge, it is you.
>
> I was so very happy to hear that you had regained some movement on your right side. That's the encouragement you need to keep motivated. Mary said both the physical therapist and speech therapist are encouraged.

You are in my prayers constantly, Uncle Phil. I look forward to hearing continued progress. I miss you terribly.

Love,
Jeanette

To a friend whose mother has a disability from a cerebral hemorrhage.

March X, 2XXX
Dear Fran:

You've frequently been in my thoughts and prayers. Although I don't know what you are feeling, I have some idea of what you are experiencing, as I also found it extremely difficult to watch my independent mother go through such massive changes as a result of a cerebral hemorrhage.

The role reversal when a parent is ill is hard. My siblings and I learned to lean on each other, and we rallied for one purpose—my mom's recovery. The reality is that your journey through life has been changed. But you have been given a precious gift: more time together.

Know that I keep you in my prayers. I will check in often and be there for you. Give your mom a big kiss for me. I'll speak to you soon.

Love,
Liz

For further information:

Albrecht, Donna. *Raising a Child Who Has a Physical Disability*. New York, NY: John Wiley & Sons, 1995.

Formulated by the Committee on Handicaps, Group for the Advancement of Psychiatry. *Caring for People with Physical Impairment*. Washington, DC: American Psychiatric Press, 1993.

Meyer, Donald J, ed. *Uncommon Fathers—Reflections on Raising a Child with a Disability*. Bethesda, MD: Woodbine House, 1995.

Mouth Magazine
Voice of the Disability Nation
P.O. Box 558

Topeka, KS 66601
www.mouthmag.com

The Ragged Edge
Ragged Edge magazine and Ragged Edge online are publications of The Advocado Press, Inc., a nonprofit 501(c)3 organization founded in 1981 to publish materials on disability rights.
www.ragged-edge-mag.com

Disability and Business Technical Assistance Centers (DBTACs)
A comprehensive resource for information on the Americans with Disabilities Act.
www.adata.org/dbtac.html

ILUSA
Directory of Independent Living Centers in the United States, typically nonresidential, private, nonprofit, consumer-controlled, community-based organizations providing services and advocacy by and for persons with all types of disabilities. Their goal is to assist individuals with disabilities to achieve their maximum potential within their families and communities.
www.ilusa.com/links/ilcenters.htm

Let's Face It
A nonprofit network that links people with facial disfigurement and all who care for them to resources that can enrich their lives.
www.faceit.org

National Council on Disability
1331 F Street, NW, Suite 1050
Washington, DC 20004
(202) 272-2004 or TTY number (202) 272-2074
www.ncd.gov

National Information Center for Children and Youth with Disabilities
P.O. Box 1492
Washington, DC 20013
(800) 695-0285, voice and TTY or (202) 884-8200, voice and TTY
www.nichcy.org

Woodbine House
Publishers of the special-needs collection.
www.woodbinehouse.com

Especially for children:
Krementz, Jill. *How It Feels to Live with a Physical Disability*. New York, NY: Simon & Schuster, 1992.

See also: WHAT IS GRIEF? UNDERSTANDING THE PROCESS OF MOURNING AND HOW YOU CAN HELP, WHAT CAN I SAY? COMMUNICATIONS THAT COMFORT, and WHAT CAN I DO? HOW TO LISTEN.

TWENTY-THREE

Separation

"Friends are made by many acts—and lost by only one."

—Anonymous

MARITAL separation ranks as one of the top three most stressful life events, after death and divorce. When couples separate, whether they plan to divorce or not, they begin a period of enormous change that necessitates a life-altering and restructuring process. Separation might come as a couple prepares to divorce, or the couple might not yet have reached that decision but are taking a break to see if they can repair the marital relationship.

Separation is an emotional time for both spouses, and although the emotions might not be as extreme as those experienced during divorce, they are very similar.

The couple enters a period of uncertainty while they must deal with the process of loss, day-to-day challenges, and problems such as changes in housing, finances, relationships, potential return to the workforce, or child care.

During this period of uncertainty and upheaval, your companionship and support will help restore stability in their lives.

THINGS TO CONSIDER

- Couples must address and deal with multiple losses such as loss of roles, security, and sense of self.

- The length of the marriage has no correlation to the depth of pain and loss separating couples experience.

- Separations might occur as a result of infidelity. The word *infidelity* conjures images of extramarital affairs, but an emotional attraction and bond with another individual can be just as damaging to the marital relationship as a sexual relationship.

- Separation and infidelity do not necessarily mean the end of a relationship. Couples can repair and heal their relationships.

EMOTIONS AND FEELINGS TO ANTICIPATE

- Agitation
- Anger
- Betrayal
- Bewilderment
- Blame
- Confusion
- Denial
- Depression
- Disappointment
- Disbelief
- Embarrassment
- Emotional turmoil
- Fear

- Guilt
- Hurt
- Loneliness
- Numbness
- Pain
- Panic
- Rage
- Resentment
- Self-blame
- Shame
- Shock
- Vulnerability

WHAT TO SAY AND DO

- Remain objective, even if they try to draw you in.

- Listen and allow the speaker to vent.

- Your job is to provide support, not to comment on their angry and sometimes hostile observations or feelings about their spouse.

> ◌ Accept what they share and what they don't. They might not choose to share with you, and this is okay.

- Encourage them to share their emotions when it feels safe and comfortable; individuals must experience the full range of grieving emotions to heal.

- Suggest that they take some time to think through their feelings and avoid making quick decisions on what they will do.

- Bring a meal or take them out to eat. Loss of appetite is very common, and they will need optimal health to work through this difficult and stressful experience.

- Include him or her in your holiday plans.

- Offer to help with child care.

- If you live nearby, help the children maintain neighborhood contacts by offering your home as the designated household for the children to play. Do this only if you will not be in the middle of custody issues.

- Respect their privacy and right for confidentiality; they might not want to make the separation public knowledge.

- Offer to help them pack, relocate, and get settled.

- Include the separated spouse in social activities such as dinners out and the movies.

HOW TO SAY IT

Can I call you next week?

How are you doing?

I am available to support you; don't hesitate to call me.

I am here if you want to talk.

I care about you.

I miss you.

I really don't know how you feel.

I will not repeat anything you say.

It's okay to feel sad. I feel sad, too.

Let me know what I can help you with.

Let's get together for coffee on Friday.

Please keep in touch.

Take all the time you need.

What can I do to help?

You can count on me.

WHAT NOT TO SAY AND DO

- Don't initiate the subject of divorce. If they want to speak about it, they will initiate the conversation.

- Don't take sides.

- Don't try to place the blame on anyone.

- Avoid saying negative things about the spouse. The couple might reconcile, and this will cause hard feelings.

- Don't play favorites.

- Avoid passing judgment.

- Don't ask for details.

- Don't suggest that they move on; they will make adjustments and move at their own pace.

- Don't fix them up with a date.

- Don't recommend a divorce attorney unless you are asked to help find one.

- Don't tell them what to do.

- Don't try and rush them through the grieving and recovery process.

- Don't measure how they are doing with someone else; everyone has their own unique way of resolving their problems, coping, and healing.

HOW NOT TO SAY IT

Didn't you see it coming?

Drop him (her).

Have you been to counseling?

He (she) was a philanderer all along.

How could you leave Sally and the children?

I never really trusted him (her).

I predicted this all along.

I told you it was never going to work.

If that's what you think will make you happy . . .

It's about time.

This is a good thing to do.

You don't deserve this.

You should have left him (her) long ago.

You should have listened to me.

Special Situations

My neighbors are separating, and I would like to retain both friendships. My children are close friends with their children.
Keep in touch with both individuals to let them know you value their friendship. Ask them how they are doing, and include them separately in family events. Inquire if they would like to be included when the other spouse is included in neighborhood social occasions. Use the children as an opening and an opportunity to continue the relationships. See the adults separately.

My spouse and I went to dinner with friends. During dinner, the husband forced his wife to confess that she is having an affair. How should my spouse and I handle the relationship with the husband, the wife, and as couples?
Sometimes the best response is no response; treat it as if it never happened. If you feel the need to help, ask the wife and husband (separately) what you can do. They might need a friend to listen or a recommendation for a good therapist.

SAMPLE LETTERS/E-MAILS

To a neighborhood friend who has separated and moved out of her home.

> January X, 2XXX
> Dear Liz:
>
> I wanted to let you know that John and I are both sorry to hear about your separation from Josh. I know things are up in the air for you, but when I said I was here to help you in any way, I meant it.
>
> It must have been very difficult for you to make the decision to move out. We are available to help you with the physical move next week; you can use our van and our muscle (or lack thereof!).
>
> I know you are worried about the kids. Bill has already told Matt that his mom and dad are separating and his mom will be moving to a townhouse where he will live part-time. I have told Matt that Bill might seem to be doing okay but he needs his friends now and he must be supportive and extra nice to him.
>
> While you and Josh work out the logistics of the separation, please keep in mind that I am willing to help watch the kids. All you have to do is call, and I will be happy to help.
>
> You mentioned your concern about feeling lonely when you won't have the kids. That could be a time when we do some fun things together. Let me think of some ideas for the next time we speak.
>
> Take care of yourself, Liz. I will call you soon.
>
> Love,
> Cate

To a friend who has been separated for several months.

> June X, 2XXX
> Dear Michelle:
>
> I was cutting flowers from the garden yesterday and came upon the pink rosebush you gave me for my birthday several years ago. It was full of blooms, and as I cut them, I thought of you and the wonderful friendship we have shared.
>
> Even though we haven't seen each other in a while, I think of you often. I

understand your desire for space and the time to sort through all the changes in your life. I would love to see you and will continue to keep in touch. No matter how you might need me, I will be here for you.

For now, the scent of these beautiful roses will keep you close to me.

With love,
Allison

For further information:

Brown, Emily M. *Affairs: A Guide to Working Through the Repercussions of Infidelity.* San Francisco, CA: Jossey-Bass, 1999.

Davis, Laura. *I Thought We'd Never Speak Again: The Road from Estrangement to Reconciliation.* New York, NY: HarperCollins Publishers, 2002.

Harley, Dr. Willard F., Jr., and Dr. Jennifer Harley Chalmers. *Surviving an Affair.* Grand Rapids, MI: Fleming H. Revell Co., 1998.

Lusterman, Don-David, Ph.D. *Infidelity: A Survival Guide.* Oakland, CA: New Harbinger Publications, 1998.

Perry, Susan K. *Loving in Flow: How the Happiest Couples Get and Stay That Way.* Naperville, IL: Sourcebooks, Inc., 2003.

Spring, Janis Abrahms, Ph.D. *After the Affair: Healing the Pain and Rebuilding Trust When a Partner Has Been Unfaithful.* New York, NY: HarperCollins Publishers, 1996.

Viorst, Judith. *Grown-Up Marriage: What We Know, Wish We Had Known, and Still Need to Know About Being Married.* New York, NY: Simon & Schuster, 2003.

Weiner-Davis, Michelle. *Divorce Busting.* New York, NY: Summit Books, 1992.

See also: WHAT IS GRIEF? UNDERSTANDING THE PROCESS OF MOURNING AND HOW YOU CAN HELP, WHAT CAN I SAY? COMMUNICATIONS THAT COMFORT, WHAT CAN I DO? HOW TO LISTEN, and DIVORCE.

TWENTY-FOUR

Divorce

"Divorce is the psychological equivalent of a
triple coronary bypass."

—Mary Kay Blakely, *American Mom*

THE dissolution of a marriage ranks as one of the most disruptive and difficult experiences, second only to the death of a spouse. Although death is a devastating experience for the surviving spouse, the bereaved usually find a wellspring of support in the community. Not so for divorcing spouses, who must go through a similar grieving process and life-changing adjustments, often with little community support.

The National Center for Health Statistics reports that 43 percent of first marriages end in separation or divorce within fifteen years. Despite the frequency of divorce, many individuals feel tremendous pain and shame and might delay telling family and friends. This tumultuous period leaves many feeling shaken, unsettled, and disoriented. The Centers for Disease Control and Prevention report higher mortality rates, more health problems, and increased frequency of risky behaviors such as drug and alcohol use after divorce.

Divorce is a major transition as individuals sever ties from their past, restructure their lives, and refashion their relationships. It might be a surprise to learn that both partners, whether they initiated the divorce or not, go through a grieving and adjustment process. For the partner who initiates the divorce and leaves, it is still a massive undertaking. Years later, some still recount painful feelings of guilt for the grief they caused their partner. For the partner who did not initiate the divorce, it can be crippling.

Many people feel a sense of failure, reliving experiences and trying to discern what went wrong. They might exert great energy analyzing past situations and actions, trying to figure out if they had said or done something different or made other choices they might have saved the marriage. They might endure sleeplessness, anger, and agitation as they try to determine who or what is to blame.

Divorce is not just the loss of the marriage; it often means the end of a lifestyle, shared relationships, financial security, future plans, and the family home. Partners lose not only a spouse, but often relationships with the spouse's family. This sad experience turns sadder when family members feel the need to take sides and once-loving family relationships turn sour.

The process of coupling leads to a merged identity, and once that couple ceases to exist, so does that identity. In an unsettled and disoriented state, individuals must find fresh identities that reflect their new status.

An adjustment to the magnitude of these changes is extremely difficult, and mental health professionals predict it takes a minimum of two years to heal from a divorce. However, each person reacts differently; for some this recovery period could take longer, and for others, shorter.

Individuals must allow themselves the time to grieve for the end of their relationship and work through the anger, sadness, fear, and sorrow. Under this cloud of stress, they might experience emotions that frighten them and their loved ones; some withdraw from family and friends and deliberately isolate themselves.

Individuals will need support from their family, friends, co-workers, and neighbors during this time period but especially during the first several months.

THINGS TO CONSIDER

- Two and a half million individuals divorce each year.

- Life will never be the same for these individuals.

- Dreams and relationships are lost.

- Forty-five percent of females have a drop in their standard of living after a divorce.

EMOTIONS AND FEELINGS TO ANTICIPATE

- Anger
- Anxiety
- Bitterness
- Blame

- Confusion
- Denial
- Depression
- Fear
- Guilt
- Hurt
- Inadequacy
- Insecurity

- Jealousy
- Loneliness
- Loss
- Pain
- Panic
- Rage
- Resentment

WHAT TO SAY AND DO

- Reassure them that they are not a failure.

- Make overtures to include them in social activities to reduce their isolation and boost their morale.

- Offer to help with meals and child care to provide stability; the transitional period before and after a divorce is particularly disorienting.

- Reassure them that anger is a very normal response, but suggest they channel their anger in positive ways such as talking it out with a friend or in a support group setting.

> ↩ An excellent way to redirect the anger is through physical activity such as aerobic exercise, jogging, walking, gardening, or painting.

- Allow them the time to become an independent, single person.

- Inquire if there is a difficult activity or chore you can help them with or get them started on.

- Suggest joining an exercise class and offer to attend with them or provide child care so they can attend.

- Recommend they keep a journal to vent emotions and establish goals. It will be helpful to maintain a steady course in their healing process and to gauge how they progress.

- Invite them to your home for a home-cooked meal and your good company.

- Introduce them to some of your friends and acquaintances to foster new relationships.

- Encourage them to share their feelings and vent their emotions.

- If there are children, volunteer to take them for a special activity to give the parent a break.

- Offer to help with carpooling. If the custodial parent is working, let them know you are available for extra turns in carpooling until they feel more comfortable in their new situation.

> ❧ Do remember them with a card on Valentine's Day or any other special holiday such as Easter, Passover, Halloween, or Thanksgiving.

- Initiate a steady date for coffee, a manicure, or a game of racquetball or tennis to offer friendship and reestablish routines.

- If you are available, volunteer to help with child care on a regular basis to ease the transition and provide some stress relief.

- Recommend they pursue participation in support groups where they can vent their feelings with individuals who share common experiences. Check your local newspaper calendars or contact social service agencies for referrals.

> ❧ An offer of child care in case of emergency is reassuring.

- Encourage them to find a support group specifically for children if there are children involved. It will be a big relief for the child(ren) to know that this has happened to other children and they are not alone.

HOW TO SAY IT

Consider me your support person; just let me know what I can do to help.

How can I help you?

I am here for you in any way you need me.

I am here to listen anytime you would like to talk.

I am so sorry this has happened.

I love you and will support you through this.

It's okay to be angry.

Please come and share dinner with me (us).

This must be very painful for you.

You're doing great.

WHAT NOT TO SAY AND DO

- Don't make negative comments about the spouse; be aware that negative comments about the spouse reflect also on children.

- Don't give your opinions.

- Don't judge them.

- Don't tell them what to do.

- Don't comment on anyone's behavior.

- Don't take the other spouse's side.

- Don't tell the partner to stop complaining and get on with their life.

- Don't throw away the photos with the divorcing spouse; ask the partner how they feel or put them away until emotions die down.

- Be very careful in front of the children; don't malign the divorcing partner or make nasty comments.

- Don't look for someone to blame.

- Don't pressure them to begin dating.

- Avoid rushing them to become a couple again.

HOW NOT TO SAY IT

But no one in our family has ever been divorced before.

But you always seemed so happy.

But you were such a great couple.

Didn't you see it coming?

Have you tried praying?

I never liked Jane anyway.

If you'd only worked less (cooked more often, had waited to have a family, etc.).

Snap out of it.

You could have made it work.

You have such a tough situation with a special needs child that no one will ever want to date you.

You should have tried harder.

You'll be sorry.

Who will be interested in you?

NONVERBAL STRATEGIES

■ The spouse who does not traditionally take care of household repairs, car maintenance, physician appointments, or laundry will appreciate help when assuming these responsibilities.

■ Offer to provide training in some task they have not had to handle before such as yard work or cooking.

■ Distract them with a movie, a sports event, a game of bowling, or an afternoon of antiquing.

■ Purchase a book or tape on meditation so they can integrate relaxation exercises into their routine to reduce stress.

Special Situations

Our neighbors have divorced, but our daughter has remained friends with their son. Our daughter is getting married soon; who should we invite to the wedding?

Invite all three of them to the wedding. Each one will have to take responsibility and decide whether they will accept or decline your invitation. Do seat all three of them at different tables, and carefully select the guests they will sit with so they can enjoy their companions and your special event.

Close friends of mine are getting divorced. How do I continue my friendship with both of them?

It is very difficult to continue relationships with both friends, but not impossible if you are passionate and committed to retaining both friendships. You'll need to be diplomatic, tactful, and nonjudgmental, not laying blame on either party nor taking sides on any issue. Although it might seem sexist, it might be more comfortable if you continue the relationship in the early stage with just same-sex activities; males participating in sports activities together and females shopping or taking in a movie. You'll need to move along with the friendship, not dwelling on what was and what will no longer be, and see what is comfortable with all involved parties. It will be essential that you support dating relationships, new ventures, and new lifestyles.

My sister-in-law had an affair and has initiated a divorce. I love my brother-in-law, and he is a terrific father to my niece and nephew. I really want to retain a relationship with him.

It is not only possible to retain your relationship, but important to do so because he will still be a big part of your niece's and nephew's lives. Keep in touch with him by phone and e-mail. If you have photos of his children, he will enjoy receiving copies along with a message from you. He is your children's uncle, so keep him updated on your children, too, because he will want to know how they are doing. If your sister-in-law is resistant, let her know that you feel it important that you foster positive family relationships for the sake of her children.

SAMPLE LETTERS/E-MAILS

To a friend who is in the process of getting a divorce.

> January X, 2XXX
> Dear Bill:
>
> It's hard to know what to say. You've both been my closest friends since college, and we have had so many great times together. I feel foolish that I was unaware that you two were having such difficulties and am so sorry to hear that you plan to divorce.
>
> There have been so many times when you have been there for me. I'll keep in touch to see how I can help you.
>
> My thoughts are with you during this difficult time.
>
> Fondly,
> Jim

To a childhood friend whose spouse has asked for a divorce.

> May X, 2XXX
> Dear Meredith:
>
> You've been in my thoughts constantly the last few days. I have truly been at a loss for what I could possibly say to comfort you.
>
> I have no experience in this area, Meredith, and yet I want to help you so much. I don't want to add to your burden, but I need your guidance so you can tell me how best I can support you and the children. Whatever you need, just let me know. I can bring a dinner, take the kids to the movies, or just sit with you and keep you company. If you want to come to my house for a change of scenery, you have an open invitation.
>
> I am so sorry this has happened, Meredith. You are a terrific person and a wonderful friend. You deserve only the best life has to offer.
>
> I will give you a call so we can make a plan to get together. Speak to you soon.
>
> Love,
> Laura

To the spouse of a girlfriend who initiated a divorce after she had an affair.

May X, 2XXX
Dear Phil,

At your wedding six years ago, I could never have imagined that I would be writing this note to you. I am so sad that your journey with Sharon as your life partner has ended. With so little choice in the matter and such painful circumstances, this must be a very hard time for you.

I trust you know how much I value our friendship and hope that we will continue to be friends. I wish Sharon had made better choices and given your marriage, which started out so strong, the time and attention it deserved.

You are a terrific person, Phil, and I wish you all the best in the future. Please take care and keep in touch.

With warm regards,
Janice

To a friend whose parents are divorcing.

October X, 2XXX
Dear John,

I was surprised to hear the news about your parents' divorce. They seemed so right together. I never thought of them individually but only as a wonderful couple.

Hearing the news brought back all the feelings I had several years ago when my parents divorced. I remember thinking, "How could it be my parents?" I also recall questioning my own ability to have a lasting relationship in the future. If my own parents were divorcing, was I destined to the same fate? These might be some of the same questions you are asking yourself.

John, this is going to be a long and challenging road. Although I still find my parents' divorce painful, I have gone on to have a happy marriage and learned from my parents' mistakes. You will, too. I want you to know that I am here for you, and I will make myself available anytime you would like to talk. I'll give you a call soon to see how you are doing.

Best regards,
Marco

For further information:

Ahrons, Constance, Ph.D. *The Good Divorce*. New York, NY: HarperCollins Publishers, 1994.

Blakeslee, Sandra, and Judith Wallerstein. *Second Chances: Men, Women and Children a Decade After Divorce*. Boston, MA: Houghton Mifflin Company, 1996.

Clapp, Genevieve, Ph.D. *Divorce and New Beginnings: A Complete Guide to Recovery, Solo Parenting, Co-Parenting, and Stepfamilies, Second Edition*. New York, NY: John Wiley & Sons, Inc., 2000.

Deits, Bob. *Life After Loss: A Personal Guide to Dealing with Death, Divorce, Job Change and Relocation*. Tucson, AZ: Perseus Publishing, 1999.

Hetherington, E. Mavis, and John Kelly. *For Better or For Worse—Divorce Reconsidered*. New York, NY: W.W. Norton & Company, 2003.

Divorce Resource Network—a guide for families in transition
www.divorceresourcenetwork.org

Especially for children:

Krementz, Jill. *How It Feels When Parents Divorce*. New York, NY: Knopf, 1988.

Lansky, Vicki. *It's Not Your Fault, Koko Bear: A Read-Together Book for Parents and Young Children During Divorce*. Minnetonka, MN: Book Peddlers, 2003.

Neuman, M. Gary, LMHC, with Patricia Romanowski. *Helping Your Kids Cope with Divorce the Sandcastles Way*. New York, NY: Random House, 1999.

Schneider, Meg. *Difficult Questions Kids Ask and Are Afraid to Ask About Divorce*. New York, NY: Fireside, 1996.

See also: WHAT IS GRIEF? UNDERSTANDING THE PROCESS OF MOURNING AND HOW YOU CAN HELP, WHAT CAN I SAY? COMMUNICATIONS THAT COMFORT, and WHAT CAN I DO? HOW TO LISTEN.

TWENTY-FIVE

Job Loss

*"Employment is nature's physician,
and it is essential to human happiness."*

—Galen

WE spend more of our waking hours at work than we do at home or with our families. Many of us devote years to planning and building our careers, studying to obtain degrees, sitting for certification and licensing exams, completing and updating our training, and taking continuing education courses. So it should be no surprise to find that many of us define ourselves by our work; our identity is what we do for our livelihood and who we do it for.

Whether someone loves or hates their job, co-workers, or commute, job loss is a disorienting experience. Daily routines are disrupted, relationships are changed, personal roles might become reversed, and financial circumstances are altered.

Employees leave jobs for many reasons, and they might receive advance, little, or no warning. Organizations might downsize and lay off staff when they are acquired, merged, sold, closed, relocated, or reorganized due to bankruptcy or a quest for greater profitability. Or they might lose funding or a contract. Employees might be dismissed for poor performance, or they might terminate voluntarily to relocate for personal reasons or due to a significant other's relocation.

But no matter why individuals lose their jobs, it is often a painful experience. Employees dedicate themselves to working toward organizational goals. They feel they make a difference and assume organizations are as loyal to them as they are to their organizations. If they find they are replaceable or the organization can easily operate without them, they mourn the loss of their value to the organization, their relationships with their co-workers, and their security.

Individuals who worked for organizations that were closed or suffered severe hardships from fraudulent business practices or dishonest senior executives will experience not only a sense of loss but betrayal as well. They might lose not only their jobs but stock value, investment funds, pension, and other benefits.

Job loss can be a frightening experience, and it is common to feel anxious. Individuals have financial responsibilities that must be maintained despite a loss or decrease in income. Families must be supported, mortgages paid, and financial commitments met.

Many individuals may be consciously aware that changes are impending after a merger, acquisition, or poor financial performance; yet many report that they still feel startled and shocked when they learn their organization will lay off staff.

Individuals experiencing job loss grieve and mourn the loss of their job, security, routines, friendships, and future. They might be in denial, unable to believe that so many people they know and care about will be out of a job. There might be anger and resentment for the lost years spent devoted to the organization and the effort exerted to climb the ladder to their current level. They might have contributed to the organization's profitability and salability, and they are justified in feeling anger, especially if the organization meets its goals and terminates staff to pursue even higher levels of profitability.

Job seekers must display confidence when interviewing for jobs. This may prove daunting to someone who has just been laid off or dismissed and is feeling like a failure. You can help to support them and boost their confidence with the right words at the right time.

THINGS TO CONSIDER

- Whether job loss is due to a major lay off or downsizing.

- Whether the organization has merged, been acquired, or closed, which might impact vested retirement payouts, severance packages, and benefit settlements.

- The number of years since the individual's last job search.

- Whether skills and experience are current.

- Whether their occupation is declining or in demand.

- Length of time they worked for their most recent employer.

- Whether they received outplacement benefits.

EMOTIONS AND FEELINGS TO ANTICIPATE

- Anger
- Anxiety
- Betrayal
- Bitterness
- Denial
- Depression
- Disbelief
- Fear

- Frustration
- Helplessness
- Insecurity
- Instability
- Isolation
- Loneliness
- Sadness
- Vulnerability

WHAT TO SAY AND DO

- Recognize the loss, and express your sympathy.

> ☞ If the job loss is due to a downsizing or layoff, assure them they lost their job through no fault of their own. Organizations go through changes, and this had to do with the organization rather than the individual, their performance, and their skills.

- Tell the person you care about them and you'll provide emotional support through the job search process.

- Allow them to feel their way through the experience and make choices in their own time and in their own way.

- Provide them with positive reinforcement on how good you think they are.

- Bolster their ego by reinforcing their talents, skills, and achievements. Job loss shakes even the most confident, and it is not unusual for someone who has lost their job to question and trivialize their accomplishments.

- Do offer to help, but don't be offended if they don't take you up on it.

- Provide advice only if you are asked directly.

- Offer to critique or proofread their résumé.

- Provide contacts through your network.

- Distribute copies of their résumé.

- Offer to role play the interview process to strengthen their interview skills.

- Purchase a job search book as a gift.

> ๛ Act as a support system, scheduling meetings for coffee or lunch to review search progress and recommend suggestions.

- Give a gift certificate to a professional résumé writer or their favorite clothing store.

- Offer to be a reference.

- Brainstorm potential employers or job search opportunities.

- Offer to provide another opinion on any aspect of the search.

- Volunteer to help with Internet research.

- Encourage them to get additional training if it will make them more marketable.

- Do return their phone calls.

HOW TO SAY IT

Fully explore your options.

Have you applied for unemployment benefits yet?

How are you doing?

I know how hard you've worked, and this must be really difficult for you.

I love you, and I'll help you in any way I can.

I'm sorry this has happened.

It's not your fault.

Take your time and find the right job.

The economy's bad; it's not you.

What can I do to help?

You are very talented, and another company will be lucky to have you.

WHAT NOT TO SAY AND DO

- Don't pity them.

- Don't ignore or avoid them.

- Don't criticize their résumé.

- Don't harass them into finding a job too quickly.

- Don't insist that they allow you to help.

- Don't pressure them into taking just anything so they will have a job; allow them to make their own decisions.

- Don't shake their confidence.

- Don't tell them they should have anticipated the layoff and been better prepared. Hindsight is always better.

- Don't blame them for quitting.

- Don't tell them this is a particularly bad time to be unemployed. It is never a good time to be out of a job.

HOW NOT TO SAY IT

Did you find a job yet?

Don't be so lazy; what are you waiting for?

Haven't you found a job yet?

I'm sure you'll find something quick.

Look on the bright side—your spouse has a job.

You better take what you can get.

You can't be too choosy.

You have nothing to worry about.

You poor thing; what a difficult thing to go through.

You'll never find the same salary.

You're still unemployed?

Special Situations

My friend keeps getting laid off.
Some industries and occupations have been particularly hard hit in the last few years. Be supportive and keep in touch. Be available to brainstorm ideas, and encourage your friend to be persistent. Invite them for dinner. Remind them that successful people succeed because they persist until they find success.

My cousin is chronically unemployed and just can't seem to stay in a job more than eighteen months.
It might be the positions or organizations your cousin pursues are not a good fit. You might encourage him to explore different types of organizations, such as federal, state, and local government; educational institutions; nonprofit organizations; corporations; or different industries. Continue to support him, and avoid making judgmental comments that might undermine his confidence in his job search efforts.

My co-worker's husband accepted a promotion, and they are relocating. Although the co-worker is happy for her husband, she is depressed because she is leaving her job and will be unemployed.
Order a subscription to the largest local newspaper in her new area so she can begin to learn the business and job opportunities in the new community. You

can also suggest you have lunch and brainstorm job search strategies. If she needs a jump start, purchase a spiral notebook and take notes for her. She will be more confident making the move and initiating a search with a notebook of ideas and an understanding of the local economy.

My friend has sixteen years of tenure with a state government and is being laid off because of budget cuts. He has only four years left to full retirement and needs to stay with his health insurer because of a previous condition. He is worried and depressed.

Encourage your friend to explore other job openings in the state, even though he might be forced to relocate or take a position with less responsibility and salary. He might not get relocation reimbursement, but it would be in his best interest to remain in the system until he is eligible for retirement. Suggest that he view the job change as an opportunity and that he maintain a positive outlook. If he finds the new job is not satisfying, he can balance his life with outside activities and community interests that will bolster his self-esteem.

My friend works for a large grocery chain that has been bought out by a larger company. He has not been laid off, but he was offered an incentive package to voluntarily leave. He has worked for this company since high school graduation and has no further education. My extensive network is in a different industry, and I think he would do well there.

Introduce your friend to key people in your network and make some calls to hiring personnel in your organization. Your friend should make the initial contacts to schedule interviews, but you can provide background information on the organization and culture prior to his meetings. It would be helpful to coach him so he knows what questions to anticipate and the personalities of the interviewers. You'll lay the groundwork so your friend will be comfortable and relaxed, anticipating a positive interview experience.

The company my spouse works for has been sold three times in the last eight years and they have downsized four times. My spouse keeps getting lucky, but I am afraid his luck is about to run out.

When you are working for an unstable organization or industry, it is imperative that you remain ready to enter the job market. Encourage your spouse to update his résumé, activate his network, and hone his job search skills. He should apprise his network members of his organization or industry instability and communicate what opportunities interest him. Suggest he continually explore and pursue job opportunities, and be prepared to move when an offer presents itself.

SAMPLE LETTERS/E-MAILS

To a former co-worker who has been laid off.

> January X, 2XXX
> Dear John:
>
> I was sorry to hear about the layoff at XYZ Company. I know you worked hard on the expansion project, and it is disappointing that things didn't work out the way you anticipated.
>
> Whatever you need, John, I'll be here for you. I can link you up with some of my contacts or set up a meeting for you with the sales manager. Feel free to use me as a reference.
>
> I will call you next week to see how you are doing and schedule a lunch. You are a great worker, John, and any organization will be lucky to have you.
>
> All the best,
> Tom

To a friend whose organization filed for bankruptcy and who was laid off with no notice.

> March X, 2XXX
> Dear Debra:
>
> What a shock this must be. I was so sorry to learn that Hall and Brighton is closing this week.
>
> You do a terrific job, Debra, and I would like to help you in any way I can. I will call you later this week and find out how I can assist you best.
>
> In the meantime, know that I am thinking of you and sending good thoughts your way.
>
> Fondly,
> Betty

To a cousin whose organization closed and the organization both laid off staff and merged several business groups with a rival firm; your cousin was offered and accepted a lesser position with the rival firm.

> March X, 2XXX
> Dear Malcolm:
>
> I was surprised and sorry to hear the news about XYZ. I know how much you enjoyed working there, and you have every right to be distressed over the firm's dissolution.
>
> The new position with Big Blue is good news. I hope you will soon feel as comfortable there as you were at XYZ.
>
> Although I know this position is not at your previous level, I feel confident that you will do well. Keep yourself open to new opportunities; they will soon see what an asset you are, and this move might take your career in a whole new direction.
>
> Know that I'm always here for you. I'll keep in touch, but in the meantime, if I can help in any way, please don't hesitate to call.
>
> Take care,
> Linda

To a friend who was laid off.

> January X, 2XXX
> Dear Collin:
>
> There are two sayings I frequently use when faced with difficult situations: The sun will come up tomorrow, and it's not how often you get knocked down but how many times you get back up again.
>
> My experience with two employment layoffs gives me a unique perspective on your current position. First of all, the sun will come up tomorrow. This might be hard to grasp in your current frame of mind, but you will face and overcome many feeling and emotions—self-doubt, worthlessness, and fear are among them. I remember the first time I was informed that my services were no longer needed. However the news was couched or soft-sold, it was a staggering blow. You hear none of the conversation after the "revelation." Instead, your mind races in many directions, none of which are particularly inviting. Sound familiar so far?

This blow to your ego seems crushing, but it is not! You might have self-doubts about your abilities or lack of them and question your career path to date—don't! You might feel as if you are swimming in a sea of perceived worthlessness. The key word is *perceived*. You deem yourself a failure, and fear begins to set in. Fear is healthy. You fear the inability to provide for yourself and your family, being ostracized by loved ones and friends, substantial financial setbacks, and drastic lifestyle changes. This fear is natural and simply put—okay.

Collin, you're much stronger and resilient than you think you are. You can and will handle this situation. Draw upon your family and friends for support. They all want you to succeed and enjoy life. They are in your corner. Use them openly and often. Never consider the act of turning to them to be a sign of weakness. Aren't you pleased when someone approaches you for help or advice? You will learn, improve, and flourish from this experience. I know I have twice!

In closing, my friend, you've been knocked down hard perhaps. But get up, brush yourself off, and figure out a plan of action with your head held high. There's no time for self-doubt, no place for self-worthlessness, and your fears are slowing abating. It's time to start a new chapter in your life. It will take courage, pride, and action. You have the first two already. Just add the third and don't look back.

I'm here for you! All the best,
Ted

For further information:

Bolles, Richard Nelson. *What Color Is Your Parachute?* Berkeley, CA: Ten Speed Press, 2003.

Cohen, William A., Ph.D. *Break the Rules—The Secret Code to Finding a Great Job Fast*. Paramus, NJ: Prentice Hall Press, 2001.

Critchley, Robert K. *Rewired, Rehired, or Retired?* San Francisco, CA: Jossey-Bass/ Pfeiffer, 2002.

Deits, Bob. *Life After Loss: A Personal Guide to Dealing with Death, Divorce, Job Change and Relocation*. Tucson, AZ: Perseus Publishing, 1999.

Kaplan, Robbie Miller. *How to Say It in Your Job Search*. New York, NY: Prentice Hall Press, 2002.

———. *Résumé Shortcuts*. Manassas, VA: Impact Publications, 1997.

Lussier, Don, with Tom Noteman and Donna M. Henderson, ed. *Job Search Secrets*. Lincolnwood, IL: VGM Career Horizons, 1998.

Nielsen, Niels H. *Princeton Management Consultants Guide to Your New Job*. New York, NY: John Wiley & Sons, Inc., 2003.

Podesta, Sandra, and Andrea Paxton. *201 Killer Cover Letters*. New York, NY: McGraw Hill, 2003.

Simon, Mary. *Negotiate Your Job Offer*. New York, NY: John Wiley & Sons, Inc., 1998.

Wendleton, Kate. *Getting Interviews*. Franklin Lakes, NJ: Career Press, 2000.

———. *Interviewing and Salary Negotiations*. Franklin Lakes, NJ: Career Press, 1999.

Job Resources
www.job-resources.com

Job-Hunt.Org
Website providing comprehensive listing of useful Internet-accessible job search resources and services on the web, including lists of links by category or location for job websites where you can search for a job and/or leave a copy of your résumé and websites that provide information and/or support useful in the job search process.
http://www.job-hunt.org

See also: WHAT IS GRIEF? UNDERSTANDING THE PROCESS OF MOURNING AND HOW YOU CAN HELP, WHAT CAN I SAY? COMMUNICATIONS THAT COMFORT, and WHAT CAN I DO? HOW TO LISTEN.

TWENTY-SIX

Financial Troubles

*"There is no such thing as failure for people
who have done their best."*

—Anonymous

PERSONAL bankruptcies increased 5.7 percent in 2002 and set a record at more than 1.5 million according to the Administrative Office of the U.S. Courts. While studies show that people are often pushed to bankruptcy through job loss, illness, divorce, or a call to active military duty, financial difficulty can also arise from compulsive shopping or spending, credit card abuse, or debt abuse.

Who's at greatest risk? Individuals who earn far less than their potential are vulnerable to financial problems, but individuals who earn far more than they are used to are vulnerable, too. They might have difficulty balancing their needs and newfound desires.

How you respond to someone experiencing financial difficulty will depend on your personal relationship and the underlying circumstances. You might be reluctant to offer financial assistance to a habitual spender but quite willing to help out if the financial difficulties were beyond their control. Whatever you choose to do, the right words and nonverbal communication strategies will help them through a difficult and uncertain time.

THINGS TO CONSIDER

- Fiscal responsibility and stability requires basic money management skills, including balancing a checkbook, establishing a budget, tracking income and expenses, saving, and investing.

■ Individuals must have a good grasp of their income and an understanding of how to live within their means.

■ There are financial counseling services available to resolve financial and credit problems such as budget counseling, money management services, debt management, debt consolidation repayment, mortgage counseling, bankruptcy counseling and/or assistance with bankruptcy, and public-service educational programs.

EMOTIONS AND FEELINGS TO ANTICIPATE

■ Denial
■ Embarrassment
■ Fear
■ Helplessness
■ Hopelessness
■ Incompetency
■ Insecurity

■ Instability
■ Panic
■ Self-blame
■ Shame
■ Uncertainty
■ Worry

WHAT TO SAY AND DO

■ If they haven't already, suggest they meet with a credit counselor if they have a lot of credit card debt or are in serious financial trouble. They can locate a reputable counselor through the Association of Independent Consumer Credit Counseling Agencies (AICCCA) or the National Foundation for Credit Counseling (NFCC). Find details for both at the end of this chapter.

■ If they are unable to pay off their debts and have to file for bankruptcy, suggest they locate an attorney. They can ask around for a referral or use one of the Internet sources at the end of this chapter to locate bankruptcy attorneys in their geographic area.

■ If they are experiencing other non-credit-related financial difficulties— for example, a spouse loses a partner to death or divorce and has never managed the household finances—suggest they locate a certified financial planner through the Financial Planning Association (FPA). Find details at the end of this chapter.

- Continue to socialize, but switch to low-cost activities.

- Invite them over for a home-cooked meal.

- Prepare extra food when they are sharing a meal with you, and ask if they would like you to pack some extras to take home.

- If you have traditionally shopped together in the past, suggest inexpensive activities such as going for a walk.

> ～ **Instead of going out to lunch, invite them over or offer to prepare a lunch and have a picnic.**

- Research free or low-cost social activities in your local newspaper such as concerts, gallery openings, or art exhibits.

- If you usually attend movies together, rent a movie, go to an afternoon matinee, or locate an inexpensive movie theater.

- Give them a gift card to their hair salon or a mall they really enjoy.

HOW TO SAY IT

I am so sorry this is happening.

Let me know what I can do to help.

Let's meet for coffee and talk.

Please let me help you; you would do the same for me.

This must be very difficult for you.

This really isn't your fault.

WHAT NOT TO SAY AND DO

- Be cautious in offering them money.

- Do not tell them it is their own doing.

- Do not find fault in how they handled their money.

- Don't point fingers on who is to blame; it is more productive to support them through this financial crisis.

HOW NOT TO SAY IT

How could this have happened to you?

I hope you enjoyed it while it lasted.

I told you this was going to happen.

You have to live within your means.

You should have seen it coming.

Special Situations

My sister is declaring bankruptcy, and I don't know what type of help is appropriate.
Your sister needs support while going through this difficult process. What you choose to do to help her will depend on your relationship and the circumstances that led to this very personal decision. Be frank and ask her what she needs, whether it is a loan to pay the attorney and filing fee, transportation if her car is repossessed, help in organizing her bills and paperwork, or a place to stay.

My son and his wife have an opportunity to buy a home but do not qualify for a mortgage due to credit card debt.
It is hard to see your children struggling. How you respond will depend on your personal financial situation, your relationship, the behaviors that led to their financial predicament, and their willingness to resolve the problem. You can choose from a wide range of options such as verbal support, invitations to dinner, help in organizing their financial papers, or an early disbursement of their inheritance.

SAMPLE LETTER/E-MAIL

To a friend who had a car accident and some medical bills that the insurance would not cover, and subsequently wound up with a large credit card debt.

November X, 2XXX

Dear Wendy:

I appreciate your trust in sharing such a personal experience with me. I had no idea your health insurance did not cover all your expenses from the accident. This has been a terrible burden for you to carry all by yourself. Please let Mark and me help you sort things out.

Mark is such a whiz in accounting he has offered to help you prepare a budget. He would also like to help negotiate a payment arrangement with your credit card company.

In the meantime, you have a standing invitation for dinner any night. Just let me know when you will join us, and I'll set a place. We'll do everything we can to help you stay on a course to reduce your debt. I am confident we can help you get back on track.

With love,
Angie

For further information:

Bierman, Todd, and Nathaniel Wice. *The Guerrilla Guide to Credit Repair.* New York, NY: St. Martin's Griffin, 1994.

Casanova, Karen. *Letting Go of Debt.* Center City, MN: Hazelden, 2000.

Eichhorn, Brian. *Credit Repair Made Simple.* Richmond Hill, GA: Beak Press, 2000.

Sember, Brette McWhorter. *Repair Your Own Credit and Deal with Debt, Second Edition.* Naperville, IL: Sourcebooks, 2003.

AllLaw.com
Find legal information or a lawyer in your geographic area
www.AllLaw.com

American Law Sources On-Line
Comprehensive, uniform, and useful compilation of links to freely accessible online sources of law for the United States and Canada.
www.lawsource.com

The Association of Independent Consumer Credit Counseling Agencies (AICCCA)
PMB 626
11350 Randoms Hill Road, Suite 800
Fairfax, VA 22030
(703) 934-6118
Locate a Member Agency by calling (800) 450-1794.

Financial Planning Association (FPA)
5775 Glenridge Drive, NE
Suite B-300
Atlanta, GA 30328
(404) 845-0011 or (800) 322-4237
www.fpanet.org

FindLaw.com
Locate attorneys in your geographic area.
www.FindLaw.com

National Foundation for Credit Counseling (NFCC)
(800) 388-2227 for twenty-four-hour automated office listings for an NFCC member location near you.
www.nfcc.org

See also: WHAT IS GRIEF? UNDERSTANDING THE PROCESS OF MOURNING AND HOW YOU CAN HELP, WHAT CAN I SAY? COMMUNICATIONS THAT COMFORT, and WHAT CAN I DO? HOW TO LISTEN.

TWENTY-SEVEN

Caregiver Responsibilities

"When I give, I give myself."

—Walt Whitman

MEDICAL and technological advances have increased our life span, but medical innovations do not necessarily translate into healthier lives. We are living longer, and more and more of us will need assistance in meeting the challenges of our daily lives.

In a survey conducted by the National Family Caregivers Association, more than one quarter (26.6 percent) of the adult population provided care for a chronically ill, disabled, or aged family member or friend in the year 2000. Based on the 2000 census data, that translated into more than 50 million people.

Most care recipients are elderly, but care is also provided to family members and friends who are ill, disabled, or injured from accidents as well as children unable to live on their own.

In a survey of 1,000 adults conducted by the National Family Caregivers Association, 59 percent responded that they either were or expected to be a family caregiver.

The National Women's Health Information Center reports that recent surveys indicate more than 7 million persons are informal caregivers to older adults. Other surveys found that almost 26 million family caregivers provide care to adults, age eighteen and over, with a disability or chronic illness, and 5 million informal caregivers provide care for older adults age fifty and over with dementia.

One of the most important things a caregiver can do is to take care of themselves. They will need a great deal of help, and you can play a vital role in supporting them.

THINGS TO CONSIDER

- Hospital stays continue to shorten as hospitals discharge patients more quickly.

- Both short-term and long-term situations require caregiver support. Some people become caregivers for a few weeks and others for a few years.

- Caregivers need a wide range of support.

- Caregivers need to relate to others who have been caregivers and understand the challenges and difficulties they face.

EMOTIONS AND FEELINGS TO ANTICIPATE

- Anger
- Anxiety
- Compassion
- Confusion
- Denial
- Desperation
- Fear
- Frustration
- Fulfillment

- Guilt
- Isolation
- Loneliness
- Regret
- Resentment
- Sadness
- Satisfaction
- Understanding

WHAT TO SAY AND DO

- Offer to conduct research on the illness, home health care, respite care, or alternative living arrangements.

- Volunteer to research available services for physical therapy, occupational therapy, nutritional counseling, meals, or medical equipment rentals.

- Volunteer to relieve the caregiver of responsibility for a few hours a week.

- Offer to stay at the home for an hour at a time so the caregiver can run errands.

- Suggest the caregiver make time for pleasant activities or interests and offer to accompany them to the movies, an exhibit, or a concert.

- If the caregiver can't get away to a favorite restaurant or coffee spot, bring it to them. Provide take-out treats and share with them.

> ☞ Suggest or offer to help prepare a comprehensive list of all medications, including name, dosage, prescription number, and prescribing physician. Offer to make copies for all health-care professionals.

- Encourage exercise as an outlet for stress. Offer to be an exercise buddy to make exercise a regular activity.

- If they aren't comfortable going out and leaving you as the caregiver, suggest you stay in the house while they take a bubble bath, a hot shower, and/or some private time for themselves.

- Help with outings. It is easier and more pleasant to have some company.

- If they are having difficulty getting adequate rest, take over their responsibilities for a few hours and encourage them to nap.

- Bring a nutritional food or meal. A container of homemade soup or a basket of muffins will be appreciated.

- When shopping, pick up an extra item at the bakery and drop it off for a treat.

- Bring a large container of sliced fresh fruit instead of sending flowers or a plant.

- Think of simple ways to lighten the caregiver's schedule while providing living necessities.

- Remember the patient, too. If they like reading mysteries, working crossword puzzles, watching

> ☞ If you play an instrument, bring it along. Live music will brighten any day. Or offer music to relax. Share your CDs or tapes of different types of music. If the patient is able to get about, research music programs that might be appropriate at the local high school or park.

> ↝ Offer to install a bird feeder or bird bath at a window accessible to the patient and caregiver. Watching wildlife is soothing and renewing, especially for those confined indoors.

videos/DVDs, or reading the local paper, keep them supplied.

■ Pets can relieve anxiety and reduce loneliness. If the patient and caregiver are agreeable, bring your pet over for a visit.

■ Pick up books on tape or CDs while visiting the local library. Choose interesting topics or best-sellers as a pleasurable way to pass the time.

■ Visit as often as you can. Companionship for the caregiver and the patient speeds the passage of time and brightens the day.

■ Please the senses of the caregiver and patient. Give a gift of a scented candle, bag of potpourri, wind chimes, or flavorful herbal teas.

■ Call on a regular basis just to chat.

HOW TO SAY IT

Do you need anything from the grocery store today?

How are you and your dad doing?

How can I help you this week?

I am on my way to the pharmacy; can I pick up anything for you?

I think you are doing a great job.

I would love to see you both.

What can I do to help?

Would you like some company?

WHAT NOT TO SAY AND DO

■ Don't stay away because you think you will be in the way.

■ Don't avoid a visit because you are uncomfortable with the illness or injury. Instead, research it on the Internet or at the library or ask questions. You will feel more comfortable when you know what to expect.

- Don't refer to the individual who is requiring help as a burden. The responsibilities might be difficult, but they might be perceived as an act of love.

- Don't express your opinions on what they should do with their patient.

- Don't give unsolicited advice.

HOW NOT TO SAY IT

He doesn't even know you are there.

I wouldn't want to end up like that.

What a burden you have taken on.

You should think about putting your mom in a nursing home.

Special Situations

My sister lives near my mother and is her primary caregiver. I live 1,000 miles away.

Despite your physical distance, there are many ways you can support your sister and your mom. Frequent notes, telephone calls, or e-mails will let them know they are in your thoughts. You can inquire if there is a specific chore you can take over, such as reconciling the medical bills. Your sister would appreciate an occasional note or a bouquet of flowers to thank her and acknowledge her efforts. You can volunteer to stay with your mom for specific weekends or a week or pay for respite care so your sister can have a break or take a vacation. You can also arrange to have a meal delivered from a favorite restaurant on a weekly or bimonthly basis.

My neighbor's husband had a stroke. He is totally incapacitated, and she is the primary caregiver.

There are some simple things you can do to help your neighbor. Call her before running your errands to see if you can run an errand for her at the same time. Prepare a double recipe once a week and take your neighbor a dinner. Offer to stay at her house for an hour so she can run an errand or have some private time. Recruit other neighbors to help mow the lawn or shovel snow. When you have free time, suggest a visit with your neighbor. She would probably enjoy some companionship.

SAMPLE LETTERS/E-MAILS

To a cousin taking care of your aunt and to the aunt who is terminally ill.

July X, 2XXX
Dear Aunt Gayle and Mary:

Just a short note to let you know that you are in my thoughts. I hope you are both managing well.

Summer has finally arrived here, and I suspect in your neck of the woods, too. I am happy for the warm weather and the chance to do some work in the garden. I enjoy watching the birds take a bath, and it's a pleasure to watch them pecking away at the bird feeder.

My girls have been busy with summer camp and music activities. There are several concerts coming up, and they are hard at work. They asked me to send along their greetings and good wishes.

I spoke with Sarah last week, and she said she had a good visit with you. I wish I was closer so I could see you, too. I know how much you enjoy a cup of tea in the afternoon, and when I take mine, I always think of you.

I will call in the next few days, and if my timing is off, please let me know when you will be up for a chat, Aunt Gayle. The sound of your voice always lifts my spirits.

You are both constantly in my thoughts. Know that I send much love your way.

Love,
Rosie

A grown daughter writes to her mother's cousin.

October X, 2XXX

Dear Ellie and Matthew:

I have been meaning to write to you for a while now—ever since I got your new address. The days pass so quickly that I never seem to get to all the things I'd like to do. Today is my catch-up day, and you are at the top of my list.

I understand that the move to your new home went well. I am glad for that. It must have been hard to decide to make such a big change. I know that when my mom finally made the move to a retirement community, she loved it.

Congratulations on your eighty-first birthday, Ellie. I was surprised to hear that you had passed such a milestone. My mom always spoke of you as the much younger cousin. I guess when you are children, four or five years seems like a huge difference.

I hope both of you are meeting the challenges this new decade brings. Recent experiences have shown me that sometimes we learn to appreciate the small steps and victories when the larger ones are no longer within our grasp. My mother really seemed to appreciate all the small kindnesses and comforts she received. Some of the things that used to annoy or bother her were no longer an issue. It really taught me a lesson about enjoying the moment and appreciating the things that were really important, like my kids, my husband, and even fresh air and sunshine.

I hope that each day you find some small treasure to make you smile or feel contentment.

Love,
Andie

To a former neighbor who is the primary caretaker for her terminally ill husband.

April X, 2XXX

Dear Joan:

I have been thinking of you often over the past several weeks. How are you both doing? I am finding that now that spring has arrived I am able to face the day with new energy. My garden is beginning to come to life, and today I noticed that at least one of the lupines I planted last year has decided to return. Maybe I will actually get some blooms this year—anything is possible.

Joan, I hope you are finding the time you need to take care of yourself while you are meeting Jim's needs. Caretaking is a full-time job, and you need to make sure to get help and respite so you can provide Jim the kind of care I know you want to give him. There is nothing wrong with asking for help and taking a break. And please remember, if you need for me to come and visit, all you have to do is ask.

You are a wonderful person, Joan. So many marriages fail even at the best of times, and the two of you have been there for each other through thick and thin. I know you probably have days that are difficult to get through. But I also hope you are getting a great deal of satisfaction knowing that the care you are giving Jim is irreplaceable and that he appreciates it more than you know—even if he can't tell you so.

I will give you a call soon. In the meantime, I am sending good thoughts and my love.

Hannah

For further information:

Carr, Sasha, M.S., and Sandra Choron. *The Caregiver's Essential Handbook: More Than 1,200 Tips to Help You Care for and Comfort the Seniors in Your Life.* New York, NY: Contemporary Books, 2003.

Carter, Roslynn. *Helping Yourself Help Others.* New York, NY: Times Books, 1996.

Collier, Andrea King. *Still with Me.* New York, NY: Simon & Schuster, 2003.

Cooper, Joan Hunter, et al. *Fourteen Friends' Guide to Eldercaring.* Herndon, VA: Capital Books, Inc., 1999.

Gray-Davidson, Frena. *The Caregiver's Sourcebook.* New York, NY: Contemporary Books, 2001.

Gruetzner, Howard. *Alzheimer's—A Caregiver's Guide and Sourcebook.* New York, NY: John Wiley & Sons, Inc., 2001.

McLeod, Beth Witrogen. *Caregiving—The Spiritual Journey of Love, Loss, and Renewal.* New York, NY: John Wiley & Sons, 1999.

Visiting Nurse Association of America. *Caregiver's Handbook: A Complete Guide to Home Health Care.* New York, NY: DK Publishing Merchandise, 1998.

Administration on Aging
Center for Communication and Consumer Services
330 Independence Avenue, SW
Room 4656
Washington, DC 20201
(202) 619 7501
www.aoa.gov/eldfam/FOR_Caregivers/FOR_Caregivers.ASP

Alzheimer's Association
(800) 272-3900
www.alz.org

American Association of Retired Persons (AARP) Webplace Caregiving: Finding Help
www.aarp.org/life

Caregiver.com
A print and web magazine dedicated to those caring for loved ones
www.caregiver.com

Eldercare Locator service is a nationwide toll-free service to help older adults and their caregivers find local services for seniors. It operates Monday through Friday, 9 A.M. to 8 P.M., Eastern time and can be reached at (800) 677-1116. The U.S. Administration on Aging makes part of this service available online so consumers can easily link to the information and referral (I&R) services of their state and area agencies on aging. These I&R programs help identify appropriate services in the area where the caregiver or family member resides. www.eldercare.gov

Family Caregiver Alliance
690 Market Street, Suite 600
San Francisco, CA 94104
(415) 434–3388
www.caregiver.org/index.html

Hospice Foundation of America
www.hospicefoundation.org

National Association for Home Care and Hospice's
Virtual Headquarters
www.nahc.org/home.html

National Family Caregivers Association
10400 Connecticut Avenue, #500
Kensington, MD 20895-3944
(800) 896-3650
www.nfcacares.org

See also: WHAT IS GRIEF? UNDERSTANDING THE PROCESS OF MOURNING AND HOW YOU CAN HELP, WHAT CAN I SAY? COMMUNICATIONS THAT COMFORT, and WHAT CAN I DO? HOW TO LISTEN.

TWENTY-EIGHT

Personal Disappointment

"Only those who dare to fail greatly can ever achieve greatly."

—Robert F. Kennedy

PERSONAL disappointments can be terribly painful. Individuals may covet leadership opportunities, attempt to win a competition, run for public office, or desire membership with a team. In the scheme of things, these disappointments might seem on the lower end of the "difficult times" scale, but to someone who has trained, planned, and prepared extensively and over a long time period to achieve their goal, this loss can be devastating.

Individuals study, practice, put in relentless hours, or spend exorbitant amounts of money for training, lessons, professional services, and equipment to achieve goals. They might sacrifice friendships and relationships, place themselves in debt, or miss out on other opportunities to experience and pursue their dreams. When an opportunity no longer exists or is earned or given to someone else, the private disappointment can become public knowledge.

You can help them through this difficult time by letting them know that you value them, their efforts, and their integrity.

THINGS TO CONSIDER

- This might have been the only opportunity to achieve this goal.

- Restrictions might exist that preclude the individual from making another attempt.

- They might never again have the opportunity to pursue their dream.

EMOTIONS AND FEELINGS TO ANTICIPATE

- Anger
- Bitterness
- Depression
- Disappointment
- Disbelief
- Embarrassment
- Hopelessness

- Inadequacy
- Incompetency
- Regret
- Sadness
- Self-blame
- Shame

WHAT TO SAY AND DO

- Take your cues from your personal relationship. A hug when you are together might be enough, followed with a note.

- Acknowledge how hard they have worked.

- Validate their skills and abilities.

- Express pride in all they have accomplished.

- Let them know their efforts and focus were not in vain.

- Reinforce that you value the skills and expertise gained by the experience.

- Tell them you love them.

- Let them know how special they are.

HOW TO SAY IT

Congratulations for a great job.

I am so proud that you set your sights on this goal.

I am sorry this didn't work out for you.

I am very proud of how hard you worked.

It is so important to reach for your goals, and you did just that.

You are my inspiration.

You did a great job.

You have accomplished so much.

You were wonderful, and I am so proud of you.

WHAT NOT TO SAY AND DO

- Do not trivialize their pain. Disappointments are terribly painful, especially when you have worked so hard to achieve a specific goal.

- Do not tell them to put their disappointment in perspective. Individuals have the right to grieve for their loss.

- Don't minimize their loss by telling them that what they hoped to achieve wasn't that important.

- Do not compare the loss to someone else's loss. If you do this, you are sending a message that their loss is not as significant or as painful.

HOW NOT TO SAY IT

And you hurt your leg for what?

It could be so much worse.

It's probably for the best.

Look on the bright side; you are in great physical shape now.

Look on the bright side. You have your health.

Put things in perspective; it's really not a big deal.

This is nothing in the scheme of things.

You'll get over it.

Special Situations

My best friend's fiancé broke their engagement three months before the wedding. How can I help my friend?

Console your friend and let her know how very sorry you are that her relationship has ended. You can lift her spirits with a bouquet of flowers and/or a note to let her know how very special she is and that she is loved. Offer concrete support to contact vendors and cancel the arrangements. Volunteer to review contracts to evaluate cancellation clauses, negotiate cancellation penalties, write letters, make phone calls, pick up purchased items that cannot be cancelled, or return gifts.

A friend in my writer's network had her book contract cancelled after she completed the manuscript.
Either call or write your friend a note to say how sorry you are that the contract was cancelled. Reassure her that someone liked her book idea before, and someone will like it again. If she does not have an agent, suggest she look for one or volunteer to help her locate recommendations. Offer to brainstorm ideas on how she can rewrite or repackage the material for another publisher.

SAMPLE LETTER/E-MAIL

To a niece who competed in a pageant and lost.

June X, 2XXX
Dearest Ellie:

It has been such a joy to watch you grow into the lovely young woman you have become. You worked so very hard to develop your musical talent and train for the competition. Your dedication and achievements demonstrated your talents to everyone who worked with you and got to know you.

The competition results disappointed you, and I am so very sorry. But I can't help but feel the real prize was the preparation and participation. You have shown wisdom and dedication far beyond your years. I am in awe of the innate ability to single-handedly focus that drives you to excellence. You are a real winner, Ellie, and I am so very proud to be your aunt.

Lots of love,
Aunt Leah

For further information:

Sell, Colleen, ed. *A Cup of Comfort.* Avon, MA: Adams Media Corporation, 2001.

———. *A Cup of Comfort for Inspiration.* Avon, MA: Adams Media Corporation, 2003.

Thomas, Marlo, and friends. *The Right Words at the Right Time.* New York, NY: Atria Books, 2002.

Zadra, Dan, comp. *I Believe in You: To Your Heart, Your Dream, and the Difference You Make.* Edmonds, WA: Compendium, Inc., 1999.

See also: WHAT IS GRIEF? UNDERSTANDING THE PROCESS OF MOURNING AND HOW YOU CAN HELP, WHAT CAN I SAY? COMMUNICATIONS THAT COMFORT, and WHAT CAN I DO? HOW TO LISTEN.

Index

About the Author

Robbie Miller Kaplan is a trainer and writer with an expertise in communications. She is a frequent speaker and lecturer for business, academic, community, association, and governmental organizations. She is the author of *How to Say It in Your Job Search, Sure-Hire Résumés, Sure-Hire Cover Letters, 101 Resumes for Sure-Hire Results, The Whole Career Sourcebook, Résumé Shortcuts,* and *Résumés: The Write Stuff* and is a contributing author to the *Strong Interest Inventory Applications and Technical Guide.* She holds a Bachelor of Arts in English from George Mason University and has a management background with Xerox Corporation.